To. Aisling,

GW00543503

My Tree of Life

Enjoy.

Rachel Doyle

Kindest Regards always

Rachel

Doyle.

My Tree of Life

Rachel Doyle

First published in 2023 by Marble City Publishing

Hardback edition ISBN 978-1-908943-59-0

Contents

Dedication

To the best parents ever.

John and Annie Candy, R.I.P, Mam and Dad.

To my husband, Frank, for always believing in me and our two amazing sons who are bringing the Arboretum brand to new heights. I'm so proud of you.

Thanks to my daughters-in-law, Kim and Lynda, and my five grandchildren.

To the Candy families and all my dear friends.

Rachel

Foreword

Who we are today is a product of both our DNA and how we have reacted to the various people and events we have encountered during our lives. Some call this the relationship between nature and nurture. We cannot do anything about our DNA other than thank our parents for it, but we do have some jurisdiction over how we react to and learn from our lives' events.

As we travel on life's journey, we are influenced by various people and events, but in turn we influence others. This influence often extends further than we realise. The influencing of others carries responsibilities. An interesting question to ask yourself is, What kind of a role model am I for others in my space?

When you read this book by Rachel – or Ray, as I call her – and reflect on her life's journey, you will see it has been built from a very solid DNA foundation. Her genetic potential was initially nurtured by her parents and over time by an ever-widening network. In this book, Ray is very generous in sharing with us some details of her journey, which will influence us, her readers, and in doing so she is a role model for all of us. She is influencing us to be the best we can be, irrespective of whatever humble baseline we have come from.

Ray is living proof that if you have clarity of purpose and are bothered enough about this purpose, you too can succeed in realising whatever you define as success. It is important that each of us build our self-worth continually so we are confident enough to have our own definition of success and work towards it. Ray gives us the map here in this book.

On a personal note, I too have been influenced by Ray. During our many meetings over the past twenty years, I have taken many worthwhile messages from her. The one I would like to highlight here concerns her

VISION. What you see on the ground in Arboretum today represents the VISIONARY picture she was painting for me all along over the years. The difference between Ray and many others is that she has converted this VISION into reality.

Remember that in both personal and business life, there is a price to be paid for doing and a larger price to be paid for not doing, but it's never neutral. Ray was prepared to pay the price. Knowing her as I do, I know she will still have new projects to be conquered even when on her deathbed. Good for you, Ray.

Thank you, Ray, for sharing your journey with us through the medium of this book. It will become a vehicle to influence an even bigger audience, to their advantage.

Blaise Brosnan

B. AgrSc. (Econ). M.Sc. (Mgmnt)

Author of *You are the Limiting Factor*,

Jack and *I Dare You*

Vision without action is merely a dream. Action without vision just passes time. Vision with action can change the world.

Joel A Barker, author and futurist

Prologue: If the Shoe Fits

I have always believed that if we choose the right dream and pursue it determinedly enough, it will come true. It is not a question of *if* but of *when*.

Back in November 2017 I was attending a black-tie event in the Malton Hotel in Killarney with the three most important men in my life: my husband, Frank, and our two sons, Barry and Fergal, and their wives. The occasion was the Retail Excellence Ireland Awards, the equivalent of the Academy Awards for the more than 600 movers and shakers in the Irish retail sector who were in attendance. I have always loved the event because it gives me a chance to meet old friends and, of course, make new ones.

During the awards ceremony and dinner, which followed a sociable champagne reception, the master of ceremonies, TV and radio celebrity Hector Ó hEochagáin, announced that a special award that hadn't been given to anyone in a decade was to be granted. It was a lifetime achievement award that only two people ever had received in the history of the event, namely Patrick Hanly, a Tipperary native who had become group company director of the English department store Harvey Nichols, and the late Senator Feargal Quinn, founder of the supermarket chain Superquinn. I couldn't wait to hear who was going to be next. Hector, a master at building suspense, eventually got to the moment of truth. The drums rolled …

'And the award goes to …'

There was silence for a split second and I took my eyes off Hector to scan the room. I was hoping I would get to see the expression on the face of the winner when his or her name was announced. There were so many deserving candidates at the tables nearby that I wasn't sure where to look.

'Rachel Doyle of Arboretum,' announced Hector.

Rachel Doyle of Arboretum? It took more than a few moments to sink in: Hector was referring to *me*. And before I knew it, my name came up in lights on a big screen at the back of the stage. This can't be, I thought. Surely someone would have told me beforehand. Surely they'd have given me a chance to get my hair done. Then a video started playing. I couldn't believe my eyes: Retail Excellence Ireland had made a film of the journey of my family garden centre business, Arboretum, from its first incarnation as a tiny back-garden affair to the thriving operation it is today – an enterprise with a multimillion-euro turnover employing over 175 people and welcoming hundreds of thousands of visitors each year. When the video ended, a spotlight focused on me and it was time for me to go up to the stage and make a speech.

A knot formed in my stomach and twisted tight. Although I had spoken at conferences all over the world, often using interpreters, I hadn't fully shaken off the shyness that had affected me as a child and young adult – a shyness that had once made me physically sick when pushing myself to give my first gardening classes. To add to my panic, as I hadn't dreamt of winning an award, I had kicked off my uncomfortable high-heel shoes and they were now under the table, buried under goody bags we'd been given on our arrival. In my consternation, I couldn't find them, and I was all too aware of how unseemly it would look if I crawled under the table to carry out a search. After all, cameras were flashing and there were 600 pairs of eyes on me. Barry, who was sitting right beside me, picked up on my dilemma and came to the rescue. Before I knew it, he had my shoes on my feet and I was click-clacking nervously up to the stage to thank the many people who had helped me in my long career.

And there were more people to thank than I could possibly remember. I'm so grateful to all those who paid beautiful tributes to me on the night. I was completely overwhelmed by the testimonials given by wonderful people for whom I have so much respect, including the then Taoiseach, Leo Varadkar. It was a night I'll always remember – a dream come true.

This book is about how I pursued my dream. More specifically, it is about how I fought hard to make it come true, in spite of the many obstacles I encountered along the way, from destructive flood water to devastating family illness. Writing this book has made me reflect on the decisions I took in both my personal life and my business, which have always been intertwined. It has also helped me to acknowledge the wonderful people who have given me encouragement and space on my life's journey and identify some of the core values that have served as my guides. My hope is that when you read my story, you will be inspired by some of the values, decisions and ideas that have made me what I am and will, in turn, achieve some of your own ambitions, regardless of your current circumstances or background.

Looking back at my childhood and at what might have been expected of a woman with my background, I often think about how things might have turned out so differently for me. I love proving people wrong.

The Early Years

The Tree of Life (Adansonia digitata)
Also known as Boabab or Reniala, this is a
prehistoric species dating back over 200 million years.
Reniala means 'Mother of the Forest'. The largest
baobab was recorded in Madagascar in 2018 and has a
girth of 28.8 metres.

When I first learned to count, I discovered that Clonmore, the little village where I was born, had two pubs, two grocery shops, two churches and two schools. It also had a post office, which is now gone. I didn't realise then that my village, being in a remote corner of northeast Carlow, was what I'd forgive you for calling a backwater. Nor did I realise it wasn't always that way. The traces of an early-Christian monastery, founded by St Mogue in the sixth century, and the impressive ruins of a thirteenth-century castle where I used to play hide-

and-seek with my friends testified to a settlement that was once all go.

Rumour had it that there was an underground passage running for a mile from the ruined castle to a nearby moat, an enchanting place overgrown with brambles and tangled trees. My friends and I spent many hours looking for this passage and dreamt of all the treasures we would find there. Alas, we never found them, nor, to the best of my knowledge, has anyone else. The treasures of my youth were to be of a different kind.

My upbringing was a lesson in resourcefulness. I was born in July 1952, the fifth child of John and Annie Candy. My older siblings were Mai, who is now deceased, Pat, Jimmy and Nancy, and the baby was John. We lived in a two-up, two-down cottage on an acre of land beside the village. This cottage was referred to as a vested cottage, which meant it was owned by Carlow County Council but could eventually be bought out by a tenant. Dad and Mam paid the council a regular rent and eventually came to own the property. I remember the celebrations when that day came although I didn't understand its significance. The house was a basic structure, but Dad, being an accomplished handyman, was able to build on extra rooms, divide others and eventually add on a porch. We collected rainwater in a large tank, and this was used for washing and bathing. We needed to have a large amount of water ready on Sunday evenings as my mother did the washing on Mondays. Drinking water was brought daily from a local well over the lane, about 500 metres away. This well was fed by two bubbling springs, and its water was crystal clear and fabulous to drink. There were ten steps down to a granite slab from where a single swoosh of a bucket could fill it three quarters of the way to the top.

My father worked long hours as a builder's labourer for Duffy's, a large business in the nearest town, Hacketstown. Duffy's had a mill, sold hardware, groceries and clothes, and had a bakery and an abattoir. For an extra few bob, Dad occasionally worked in a piggery in Tinahely. I can still remember feeling sorry for him as he tried to wash away the foul stench of the pigs when he came home.

One day a fire broke out in the hopper of the grain dryer in Duffy's and Dad suffered severe burns as he ran through the flames to close the great door of the vault. He managed to contain the fire but had to spend several weeks recovering in hospital in Baltinglass. I recall my mother hiring a car to take me and my siblings to visit him and how shocked I was to see his face blackened with scars. It is an indictment of the time and the way workers were treated that he was not paid for his time in hospital. While I believe the unions of today can sometimes push too far and have become too powerful, I believe that had Dad been in one, he might have been treated better after his accident. Our local shop gave us food on tick when he was in hospital because no money was coming into the house. We were lucky in that we had our own vegetables and fruit in storage – from root vegetables to rhubarb – so we never went hungry, and my mam could conjure up a tasty meal from next to nothing.

Today people often inquire how I first got into gardening. My response is simple: I was born into it. Each evening when Dad would cycle the three-mile journey home from Duffy's, he would work in his beloved garden and I would watch closely as he grew and harvested the fruit and vegetables that kept us practically self-sufficient throughout the year. I learned so much from him by osmosis.

The feast day of Saints Peter and Paul, 29th June, was special in our household, not only because it was a Church holiday but also because it was the day on which the first of the new potatoes were dug up. It was like a ritual in the house. The potatoes were washed, cooked in a large pot of boiling, salted water and served up to us with knobs of melting butter. They were delicious, and their taste stays with me to this day. Sometimes we mashed the potatoes and added chopped spring onions. These too were served with butter, which was very often homemade.

Some potatoes from each year's crop were kept as seed for the following year. Sorting the seed potatoes with Dad and cutting them up for planting, making sure that there was an 'eye' or bud in each piece, is a memory that has remained with me. The varieties I remember were Kerr's Pinks, British Queens, Aran Banners, King Edwards and Golden Wonders. The Aran Banners were grown because the tubers were large and good for the pigs. After harvesting, the potatoes were kept in a specially constructed pit.

I can still recall the special flavour of our root vegetables, especially the young carrots. As children we would often pull them out of the soil and eat them raw. Dad used to complain to Mam that the 'rabbits' were in his garden again and had eaten his carrots. We thought he genuinely didn't know who the real culprits were. The carrots, along with parsnips, were stored in a pit. Potatoes were in another pit. Turnips and swedes, on the other hand, were stored in the shed, along with hanks of dried onions.

My mother would often ask John to take a breadknife to cut a head of cabbage for dinner. John would insist that I help. It was my job to hold back the head of cabbage so he could get close to the stem and cut it, which he did. Years later he revealed that he needed me to help because he was afraid he might hurt a baby. We were told that babies were found under a head of cabbage! The innocence of country children back then.

I remember Dad's first apple tree. In its first season, it produced only one apple. Dad warned us not to go near it because he wanted to assess its flavour when it ripened, but my brother Pat climbed the tree and ate it *in situ* without pulling it off its branch. He later assured

Dad that the flavour was good. It must have been good because we eventually had delicious, crunchy apples of all varieties in the garden. The Bramley, Worcester Pearmain and Egremont Russet apples were packed in crates and kept in the shed.

Dad also grew spinach, a vegetable that wasn't very popular in those days, but he believed it was a good source of iron for growing children. He picked nettles from the hedgerows, knowing they too were rich in iron. We were fed three servings of them in the month of May and they were cooked like cabbage and served up to us with melted butter and comments that they were good for us. Dad grew many types of brassicas, including savoy cabbage, greyhound cabbage, Brussels sprouts and cauliflower, in addition to lettuce of all types.

Dad always used twigs from ash trees that grew in the hedge around the garden as dividers between different varieties of vegetables. These twigs would, over the season, produce fresh, white, succulent roots and grow on as young trees. I was fascinated that it was so easy to grow a new tree. Years later I would find myself working with kids from a local school for children with special needs only to be thrilled that they shared the sense of excitement I had experienced as a child on seeing the magic of seeds and cuttings producing their first roots and shoots.

I remember being with Dad in Drummond's establishment in Carlow. This was an old-style shop where seeds and many horticultural implements were sold. Memories of Dad's conversations with the man who sold the seed have stayed with me all my life. Dad collected seeds from an impressive variety of plants, and I particularly liked the lupin seeds. I would gather them when ripe, store them in boxes over the winter, sow them in the spring and watch them grow. This is something I still do. I also collect the seeds of nasturtiums and night-scented stock. For me this is an exercise in nostalgia in that it brings me back to my happy, carefree childhood.

From May 1939 to July 1945, Dad had served in the Irish Army. He was very proud of his service. He credited the Army with instilling in him a strong code of practice. It taught him how to dress impeccably and to be punctual always. In addition, it taught him many life skills, such as cutting hair, mending shoes and repairing saucepans and bicycles. These practical skills complemented his talents in other areas, among which were his cardplaying. We were a family of good card players and, even now when members of my family gather together at Christmastime, the tradition lives on.

We had one of the first battery-operated radios in the neighbourhood and it took pride of place in the kitchen – the centre of the house where everything happened, from meals to prayers and homework. The radio attracted all the neighbours in regularly to listen to the Sunday football match. The distinctive voice of the commentator, Micheal O'Hehir, was known and admired throughout the land. The evening news was another popular programme and the weather forecast was often the most important item.

Dad was a singer, dancer and poet. Where the latter talent is concerned, I recall Mam showing me a story about him that was published in the local newspaper's report on courthouse proceedings. It stated that, in one of his specially composed songs, he had mentioned a local man who was easily identifiable and who was not too thrilled with how he was portrayed. The man had sued for slander. The judge threw out the case and said the locals should be proud to have a 'bard living amongst them'.

In October 1974, when I was a young adult, Dad was contacted by Tom Munnelly and Danny Brown from the Irish Folklore Commission, which is now housed in University College Dublin, with a view to making a recording. Dad contacted three of his friends – James J.

Byrne, Paddy Kelly and Mick Donoghue – and a recording session was arranged. They sang some old traditional songs and a few of Dad's own compositions. I can clearly remember the excitement in the household when they were informed the recording would be featured on RTÉ radio. Word quickly spread around the area and our house was full of neighbours on the night of the broadcast. We were very pleased when the archive department of RTÉ gave us a copy of the recording. It is one of our most treasured family memories.

My mother, like many women at the time, kept the house. She was shy but very hospitable to visitors. She made jam from the fruits of the garden and the hedges and was a natural cook who never needed to weigh ingredients or measure when baking. She kept seven different tins and on occasions each contained a different kind of cake. Just as I saw magic in Dad turning broken twigs into trees, I saw magic in Mam turning raw ingredients into cakes or soda bread. It was rare for us to be given what we called 'shop bread', and tinned beans were considered luxuries to be served only occasionally as special treats. Mam's homemade bread was a staple in our household, and boxty – a dish made with potatoes, flour and buttermilk – was a special treat. I love cooking and would consider myself to be a good cook but I cannot make brown or white soda bread as good as Mam's.

Our home was an open house. When neighbours called in, there was always a cup of tea and Mam's speciality, a version of soda bread with butter, eggs and currants or raisins, known as spotted dick. Mam was always pleased when it was praised, and this happened often. Frequently, our dinner was shared with whoever happened to call. The card games were a regular night-time feature in our home and, again, the visitors joined in. Mam never played and was happy to make the tea and the sandwiches and pass around her marmalade cake, which was always kept in a special tin.

Recipe and method for Mam's marmalade cake

4 oz (113 grams) butter

4 oz (113 grams) sugar

2 eggs

A little milk

2 tablespoons marmalade

6 ozs (170 grams) flour

1 tsp baking powder

Beat the butter and sugar until white and fluffy. Add the eggs, milk and marmalade. Sieve the flour and baking powder into the mix and fold until the flour is mixed through. Pour into a greased loaf tin and bake at 180°C for about 45 minutes.

Although my mother taught me how to cook, I never mastered her ability to assess quantities of ingredients without mechanical aids. You can imagine my joy, then, on getting a weighing scales from Santa one Christmas. However, I had the scales for only a few months when my brother Jimmy decided he would like to see how they worked. He took them apart and they never worked again. Even then, as now, I could never be annoyed with him; he is one of nature's true gentlemen.

Mam was proficient at making clothes and quilts. She repaired our clothes using only needles and thread, and those clothes that were beyond repair she turned into bedspreads. She had no sewing machine. She would darn socks and alter hand-me-downs. I would help her in these endeavours, and I learned from her at an early age how to make clothes and manage a household. She was a recycler before the current trend.

My aunt Rachel, after whom I was named, lived in the USA. She used to send us hand-me-downs from my cousins. I can remember the excitement when the big box arrived. The contents always seemed to have a particular fragrance. I'm sure it was only fabric conditioner but to me it was the scent of America. One of the items sent to me was a dress for my First Communion, but I remember not being impressed. It was pale pink and I wanted it to be white like everyone else's. Despite my protests, I wore it and slowly came to think it looked good. Having said that, I looked forward to the day when I would have enough money to buy my own clothes. That opportunity would come soon enough.

Rachel's Reflection

'Waste not, want not' was the code by which we were reared. Everything possible was recycled, reused and renewed, and waste was reduced.

Industrious Beginnings

The Rowan or Mountain Ash (Sorbus aucuparia)
Also known as 'The Lady of the Mountain'
The old Celtic name for the Rowan translates as wizards' tree. In past times it was grown around churches, in graveyards and close to homes to ward away evil spirits.

Each morning we were treated to the sound of a milk van labouring up the road and turning in to our little cottage in Clonmore. The van belonged to Ben McCall, who owned the grocery shop in Hacketstown. The milk was transported in several large churns, the smallest of which had a capacity of 40 litres and a spout. The volume we wanted was transferred from the small churn to our milk bucket by means of the spout. Ben also brought us flour in large cotton bags. Later, these were recycled by my mother for use as pillowcases or tea cloths, or sewn together to make the inside of patchwork quilts. The top layers of the quilts were made from clothes no longer considered fit to be worn and which were cut into patches and stitched together.

It was in the shop of Ben McCall that my brother Pat, my sister Nancy and I got our first part-time jobs. I was about thirteen when my turn came. It was work that I would continue to do on Saturdays, for a half day on Sundays and during holidays throughout my teenage years. McCall's shop had no till. Instead, we had a book in which every transaction was recorded and where the money received was totted up at the end of each working day. This is a practice that I still adhere to, even if I use more modern methods to keep track.

At the back of the shop, pig meal, bone meal and layers mash for hens were weighed out in the quantities required by the customers. Tea and sugar were also weighed out, and even biscuits were sold loose. There was no complicated packaging then. Food was packed into brown paper bags rather than the plastic-covered polystyrene trays we see today, and people brought their own hessian shopping bags with them when going shopping. I worked in the shop until eleven o'clock every second Saturday night, stayed overnight and on Sunday mornings washed the floors, dressed the McCall children and cooked breakfast for the family. The shop opened in the morning after eight o'clock Mass and was always busy with people who lived some distance out in the countryside. These people used their trip to Sunday Mass as an opportunity to do their weekly shop. When I had the shop floors washed and polished, I would head off for Mass at eleven o'clock and return afterwards to serve customers. In the afternoon I would walk the three miles home to Clonmore.

From Ben McCall and his wife Mai, I learned not only about retail but also about customer service. I grew to love the interaction with the customers and salespeople. While I was glad of the pocket money, much of which I spent on clothes, I was delighted to be learning about the retail trade. I took a keen interest in what was being sold and kept an eye on what wasn't selling well. Although I was shy, I got on so well with Ben that I was happy to chat away with him and ask questions.

'Why are we stocking Zebraline?' I once asked, curious to know why he bothered to stock a brand of grate polish that hardly anyone ever bought.

'There's the odd person who comes in who wants it,' he replied.

'I suppose you're right,' I responded, not fully convinced.

Shortly afterwards, I asked Ben the same question about pigmeal, layers mash and bonemeal. His answer was much the same, although this time he added that his shop was the only place around where you could get those products. He didn't want his customers going home empty-handed. I was happy with that. It hadn't fully dawned on me that there was more to retail than merely making money. I like to think that it is because of Ben that, in Arboretum today, we carry unusual and rare plants to facilitate the small few who want them, even though they don't fly off the benches.

When I had thought about Ben's views on customer service, I plucked up the courage to make a proposal to him.

'You know when we're standing here and there's no customer about?'

'Yeah?'

'Can I go to the store at those times and weigh the half stones of bonemeal and layers mash?'

'That's a great idea,' he said.

I could see he was proud that I was taking the initiative. I thought weighing the produce was a really important job and was delighted to be given the responsibility. Just like today, I didn't want to be standing around doing nothing if there were no customers to serve or shelves to be stacked. I wanted to be doing something useful. Little did I know then how much my first retail experience would benefit me in my twenties, when I would open the doors of my first garden centre.

***

Fuel was an important consideration for us at home in Clonmore because we needed it not just for warmth in the winter months but also for cooking food. As with the vegetables, we provided our own. It was a job for all the family. We had a turf bank on Jones's bog. Dad used to cut the sods with a special instrument called a sleán, which was like a spade with two sides. Using it was challenging and only some men mastered the art, but my Dad was considered an expert. When each sod was cut, it was tossed to a barrowman – usually one of my older brothers – and each barrowful of turf was emptied on flat ground and left there for a few weeks to dry.

The next step was a process that we called 'footing'. This involved standing the sods upright and leaning them against each other – with each stack having five or six sods – so the wind could dry them out further. This was backbreaking work for adults, and we children had to do our share too. When we were quite small, my little brother, John, and I – and also Nancy, but to a lesser extent – usually got away with doing less than my older brothers because we very often broke the sods when we were trying to get them to stand against each other. Perhaps there was method in our madness. I probably just got in the way. Dad frequently sent me to pick the bog cotton to bring home to my mother, probably so he could get on with his work and avoid the questions that I asked constantly. After a few weeks, depending on the weather, the footed stacks of turf were arranged into slightly larger stacks, which would spend several more weeks on the bog drying out further.

On summer evenings at turf-saving time, my father would go directly to the bog from work and we would join him, bringing with us his supper, which consisted of tea and sandwiches made by my mother. If the vacuum flask was broken – it frequently was – the tea was put in a lemonade bottle and kept warm by wrapping it in a knitted woollen sock. Nothing ever tasted as good as the tea and food consumed on the bog, and my father was always generous in sharing his supper with us. We all loved to be on the bog though the work was hard and sometimes tiring, and we had to be very careful not to wander away in case we stepped into a bog hole. Some of the bog holes were up to six metres deep and filled with water.

In the autumn we all got a day off school to help stack the turf in our big shed after it was brought from the bog on a lorry. Mam provided the food for the feast that followed and Dad used the opportunity to invite the neighbours over for a singsong. Saving the turf was an education in neighbourliness and co-operation.

Winters could be difficult in the valley when the snows came. We could be cut off from the nearest town for days at a time, so it was important that we always had enough turf for the fire and flour for the bread. Nothing in our house was wasted. We kept three pigs, which were fed from the small potatoes and the leftovers of the household, serving as another good example of recycling. The pigs were fattened and brought to market to provide money at Christmastime.

Notwithstanding that money was scarce in our family, we were well cared for. We had a happy home. Although my brothers, Nancy and I all helped out at home, in the garden and at the bog as children, we had time to play and enjoy our childhood. We often derived fun from foraging, although we didn't know the word at the time. I have fond memories of all of us going off to pick mushrooms. They had an amazing taste, nothing like the forced products of today. Then again, the wild mushrooms are quite different in their make-up from the ones we buy in the shops. We picked bucketloads of the juiciest blackberries when they were ripe and Mam used them to make many kinds of desserts and jams. I can still remember the distinctive tang of her apple and blackberry jam. We also gathered what we called 'fraocháns' – wild bilberries that grew on the bogs – when they were ripe. They made great pies. There was a wealth of nature's bounty available to us that nobody knows how to use today. It saddens me to see the ecological equilibrium is now upset and that biodiversity is in decline. When I was a child, our garden was always full of hedgehogs, which helped to deal with the snails, but now there are few to be seen.

While it is obvious to me that my upbringing made me a resourceful, industrious person who looks to the natural world for so many things, it is only in writing this book that I see that, as a child, I was exposed to something else that would assist me greatly in later life: creative garden design. As well as growing vegetables and fruit, my dad kept a pretty, ornamental garden. Although he had never travelled abroad and had certainly never seen a topiary garden, he took time away from growing vegetables to train his shrubs to grow into extraordinary shapes – creations that could have come only from his inventive imagination. Or perhaps he had seen such things during his younger days as a soldier. On the other hand, my older brother Pat, who had a keen interest in topiary, may have influenced Dad in the art. Dad was a good teacher and it was from him that I got my love for ornamental plants.

Muintir na Tíre is a national voluntary organisation devoted to the development of the community. I recall that in the 1970s it organised a garden competition. Dad won the first prize for his garden in 1974, 1975 and 1976, his plants having been grown from slips and collected seeds. He was given a cup in 1974, and when he won the competition in the two subsequent years, he was allowed to keep it. He was so proud of this award. My brother John gave me this cup when Dad died, and I treasure it to this day.

On occasion, during the summer holidays, Dad would hire a car and take the family out to the beach or the mountains for an outing and a picnic. We always had a day out on St Patrick's Day at the point-to-point horse-racing in Shillelagh, County Wicklow. When Pat got a car, these outings became more frequent. I remember them with great fondness.

My parents were typical of the working people of 1940s and 1950s Ireland. They had no formal education. They spent a few perfunctory years at national school, but very often the exigencies of home life kept them from school for days or even weeks at a time. Secondary education was the preserve of those who could afford to pay for it. Free secondary-school education was introduced in Ireland only in 1966. My mother was content with her lot, cooking, sewing and generally caring for her family, but my father thirsted for knowledge. This is evident from his many talents, some of which I have already mentioned. He could extend a house and repair broken implements, and he was also the local barber, shoemaker, vegetable grower and entertainer. He could sing and dance and compose songs, but he couldn't spell and would often ask me to write out his poems and songs because he was embarrassed to do it himself. From an early age, I was conscious of the educational shortcomings that disadvantaged him, and I was determined not to end up in the same boat. I was resolute in deciding I would have the best education I could manage.

Ours was a religiously mixed community. Our family was Catholic and our nearest neighbours, namely Mr Proctor (we always called him 'Mister') and his sons, were members of the Church of Ireland. They would frequently visit our house to listen to the radio or just chat. When Mr Proctor died, I remember standing beside my younger brother, John, looking over the gate at his headstone in the Church of Ireland cemetery and in our childish, naive way feeling sad he was not in Heaven because he was a Protestant. I also remember that his daughter-in-law asked Mam if I could help out at his wake. She agreed, so I was given the task of making the farmer's butter. This was a big responsibility that I was so proud to be trusted with. I made perfect butter and shaped it with the butter pats, also known as Scotch hands. It was well received. It was a lesson for me in giving people responsibility and trusting them to rise to the challenge. People need space to develop.

The rural electrification scheme didn't reach our part of County Carlow until late in 1962, when I was ten. The erection of the poles in our locality started in March 1961 and the electricity was switched on for us in

January 1963. Until then we had lived with Tilley lamps for light in the evenings, a turf fire for heating and a range for both heating and cooking. The nearest town, Hacketstown, had electricity before we did.

My older brother Pat was one of the bright sparks of the family. Even when I was a child, I admired his tendency to read everything he could about a subject to become proficient in it. Today I would describe him as having had an entrepreneurial mindset. Like his father, he knew the names of plants that few other humans knew. At one time he wanted to go to the Botanic Gardens to study but he was not allowed. To Mam and Dad, Dublin seemed a million miles away.

Pat was a genius with wiring and lights, in which he was self-taught, and ran a two-core flex from the battery-operated radio in the kitchen to the corner of the adjoining sitting room. His friend, the late Paddy O'Gorman, gave him a high-frequency speaker to attach to this flex. The speaker could double up as a microphone when the radio tuner was adjusted to receive the signal from it. Pat would prepare fake news bulletins that purported to report on various events in the neighbourhood. One of these was about a problem at the Poulaphouca water reservoir and another about a recent general election. His report on the election stated that none of the declared candidates had been elected to the Dáil and it gave an entirely different list of elected Members. This was followed by a cattle-market report outlining a catastrophic drop in prices. Another report was about the dangers associated with Poulaphouca electricity-generating station, and a warning was given that it was dangerous and could kill us all.

On several occasions, Pat broadcast his outrageous reports when two of our neighbours were in the house listening to the news. They really believed every word that came from the radio was true – even Pat's reports – and decided they would have nothing to do with this new-fangled and dangerous electricity. On another occasion Pat announced he was handing over to Cork Opera House as a famous singer was about to perform the song 'Oh to be in Doonaree'. I started to sing and it didn't take long for one of our neighbours to say, 'Turn that radio off. She sounds like a cat pissing against galvanise.' It certainly put an end to any thoughts that I had a future as a soprano.

Our two visitors went to the local pub and related all the things they had heard on the radio. Their drinking friends assured them that the Candy family had a different radio, and different news, from everyone else.

Clonmore is still very dear to me. My visits there now are mainly to visit the graves of my parents and see the Kinsella family, friends from my childhood days. My younger brother, John, who has inherited Dad's love of composing songs and poems, has written some poems and songs about the village that echo my nostalgia. One, called 'Clonmore', goes as follows:

There's a spot in north-east Carlow.
It's a place with great renown,
Close by the Wicklow border, just three miles from Hacketstown.
It's an ancient little village steeped in history and folklore.
Sure it's there I spent my childhood, in the village of Clonmore.

Fond memories come flooding back – in my mind I see them still,
Of the moat above the village on the road to Eagle Hill.
The castle ruin and the old schoolyard I remember oh so well,
The Bullawn stone, the old stone cross, and Saint Mogue's holy well.

My thoughts drift back in history when
Cromwell was our foe.
He marched upon this hallowed ground
and our castle he laid low.
These facts are etched in history and
will remain forever more,
Of the hardships that were once
endured by the people of Clonmore.

As we pass down the Chapel road, it's
the place I know the best,
Past the Chapel and the graveyard
where my parents take their rest.
There we stop awhile and bend our
knee, as we did in days of yore,
At Our Lady of the Wayside church in
the village of Clonmore.

Then up to Killalongford hill, a place I still recall,
Where once lived the ancestors of the great P. J. McCall,
He who penned some mighty ballads, Boolavogue and many more,
He will forever be remembered by the people of Clonmore.

There are many places in this land that some may call the best,
But there's a spot in County Carlow that outshines all the rest.
It's the ancient little village that I long to see once more,
And someday I know I will return to the village of Clonmore.

From *Rambling Down Memory Lane* by John Candy.

Rachel's Reflection

From an early age, families worked hard together, learned together and celebrated together. This has served me well in growing Arboretum with my family.

If I Knew the Answer

Apple (Malus pumila or M. domestica)
Apple, known as 'The Tree of Love', and
'The Paradise Tree', is associated with Aphrodite, the
goddess of love. The apple is associated with good
health and happiness.

One of the great regrets of my life is that I left primary school without a basic education. I attended a small, rural, two-roomed, two-teacher school with a large turf fire in each room and an outside toilet. We children gathered sticks to light the fire each morning. Each teacher had to teach four classes. Although I was thirsty for knowledge and education, even at an early stage in my life, I have always felt that my teachers concentrated more on those children whose parents could afford to send them to secondary school. While the religious orders who were involved in schools could be generous in accommodating some children by way of scholarships, it was not considered to be part of my future. I was an extremely shy child and when asked to name the capital cities of various countries my brain would go blank from fear. Even if I knew the answer, I couldn't speak. I can still remember clearly the varnished blackthorn stick.

During the big snow in January 1963, my mam walked to my primary school to take my sister Nancy, my brother John and me home because her father had passed away. When travelling to our grandfather's funeral in Tinahely, we were intrigued by the huge snowplough as it moved the drifts of snow aside to make it possible for the hearse and our hired funeral car to make the journey. In our childish innocence, we thought it was great fun and didn't understand that this was all very traumatic for our mother, who was experiencing great loss.

When I finished in primary school, I cycled every day the three miles to Hacketstown to attend the vocational school, which was known as 'the tech'. Vocational schools were established mainly to teach technical skills while the fee-paying secondary schools of the time concentrated on academic subjects and prepared pupils for the state exams, namely the intermediate and leaving certificate exams. Passing these was necessary for entry to third-level college. Hacketstown vocational school progressed pupils only to group certificate level after two years, and to intermediate, or 'inter', certificate level at the end of the third year. I was in the first group of students who could sit the leaving cert but we had to go to the vocational school in Tullow as Hacketstown wouldn't cater for the handful of us who wanted to continue on. In time all the vocational schools would prepare students for both the 'inter' and leaving certificate exams.

When I was in my teens, my self-esteem was at rock bottom. I believed that all my school friends knew more than me, resulting in feelings of insecurity and of not being good enough – feelings that haunted me for years. I can remember a teacher going on about the *aimsir chaite* and *modh coinníollach* – tenses in the Irish language – and I had no idea what they were. I'm afraid it was all double Dutch to me. Fellow pupils who had gone to national school in mountain villages such as Knockananna and Annacurra, which were even more remote than Clonmore, seemed to me to be so much further ahead. I can make light of it now but it had a big effect on my self-esteem. It took a lot of effort for me to convince myself I was as good as anyone else and that I should believe in myself. My Dad encouraged me in this by telling me that what I was doing was right and that if I put my mind to anything, I would succeed. I put my mind to learning as much as I could and catching up as fast as I could.

'You're able to do it. Just stick with it and you'll get there,' he used to say.

On my way to and from school, I frequently got off my bicycle to admire plants by the roadside hedges, much to the amusement of my friends. In spring I would pick ferns and display them in a jam-jar in the fireplace in the unused parlour, and in May I would pick primroses for the 'May altar', a special space created in Catholic homes like ours to honour the Virgin Mary. In June I would stop to admire foxgloves because I used to love watching the bees creeping into and reversing out of their tubular flowers. Very often I brought specimens home for Dad to identify. I never knew where or how he had acquired his knowledge of plant names but he was an expert on wild flowers and plants. I particularly remember digging up a periwinkle (*Vinca minor*) that took my fancy when I saw the neat small leaves and pretty blue flowers. I brought it home and it grew well in our garden. I still love this little plant and feel that perhaps it gave me some indication of what I would like to do in later life, even though I didn't have a precise sense of the possibilities open to me.

When I had successfully completed my three years in the vocational school and obtained my 'inter' certificate, I had to make my way to the larger town of Tullow, where it was possible to study for the leaving certificate, which I was determined to attain. There were no career guidance teachers in schools at the time. As my family and I assumed I would end up working in a local office after school, I reluctantly decided to take accountancy and business as my subjects instead of my preferred ones – chemistry and biology. Since it was expected that girls like me would get married and have children and therefore not have much need for education, we were told to take subjects at pass level, but I decided I would do home economics, accountancy, business studies and art at honours level. I suppose I was a bit of a rogue in that I didn't always do what was expected of me. Besides, I had to honour my promise to myself that I wouldn't suffer an educational disadvantage.

It was a long journey each day to and from school in Tullow. I would get a bus at twenty past seven in the morning and it meandered through the villages of Hacketstown, Kiltegan, Tinock, Tinahely, Carnew and Shillelagh, picking up pupils along the way. The driver, Joe Whelan, used to entertain us, and no doubt himself, by singing throughout the journey. He is a recorded artist with a great voice and I still listen to his songs if I have to go on a long journey. He is a perfect gentleman and we have been friends ever since my youth.

I studied diligently and passed my leaving certificate exam. While I was happy with that, there was something troubling me: I regretted my choice of subjects. I felt I should have done chemistry and biology. Therefore, I decided to return to school to repeat these subjects in the leaving certificate, this time in Carlow through night classes. Again, I passed my exams. On reflection, accountancy and business turned out to be relevant to what I do today. However, education is not a load to carry.

Soon after having passed my leaving certificate exam, and against my parents' wishes, I went to London with a school friend, Mairead. This was considered to be a rite of passage for many young Irish people at the time. Unemployment at home was high and Britain was prospering with post-war reconstruction. The building trade was consequently flourishing and there were many opportunities for finding work. Before leaving Clonmore for London, the man who had been my employer and mentor in the local shop, Ben McCall, approached me to say goodbye.

'Just remember Hacketstown 15 is my phone number if you need anything,' he said, putting a few bob in my hand. That was such a comfort to me because I knew there was no use in writing home for money if I needed any. I had such respect for Ben because of that gesture.

Mairead and I had arranged to stay in London with her aunt but when we arrived on her doorstep we discovered that she was away on holidays. Luckily, I had the telephone number of Mary Cummins, whose sister was married to one of my brothers. She allowed us to sleep on a sofa in her flat until we found employment and lodgings. My job was as a chambermaid in a hotel near one of the big railway stations, an area that was at the time a well-known haunt of the ladies of the night and their clients. I was an innocent abroad – a young country girl ignorant of the seedier side of big cities. I had an uncle in London at the time, Peter, and I remember raising with him the subject of the strange goings-on near the railway station.

'Some of the girls I work with go out to Knightsbridge to be picked up,' I said. 'What does that mean?'

He didn't comment, except to say I should never go with them! Some time later, he told me how relieved he had been when I had told him I was going home and that London was not for me. I returned to Carlow to a similarly relieved Mam and Dad, who had not wanted me to leave home in the first place.

Thankfully I hadn't needed to phone my old boss Ben McCall from London, but he was my first port of call when I returned. He kindly gave me part-time work until something permanent came along. I was loyal to Ben so he in turn was loyal to me. While working with Ben, I wrote to Duffy's, the company that employed my father and asked for a position in the office. Since Dad was so respected, I soon got a call from his employer, Matt Duffy. Matt invited me to go to his premises for a chat and offered me a job. This is what both my parents had desired and, indeed, predicted.

Soon after being shown the ropes in Duffy's, I found myself doing what I found to be very boring work, apart from the relative excitement of learning to use the new addition to the office – the office computer. I was the first to learn how to use it and was offered overtime to do so, which didn't go down well with my colleagues. One day, as I toiled away on entries to a daybook for the drivers, I heard the Angelus bell toll at midday and thought, 'I'm doing the same work at this time today as I was doing yesterday, and I'll be at the same task at the same time tomorrow.' It was time to move.

When I left Duffy's – very much against Dad's wishes – I found a new occupation as a substitute national school teacher in Hacketstown. I had been approached by a priest in the town, a lovely man called Fr Boylan, and asked whether I had an interest in the position. Such positions were always going to be temporary and could not be considered suitable long-term employment, but I loved the prospect of the work. Teaching turned out to be much more rewarding than the office from which I had escaped. I loved working with the children especially and was particularly proud of them when they turned out the best nature table in the school.

One day a colleague in the school, Mairead Duffy, came up to me with a copy of a newspaper advertisement from the *Irish Independent* and slapped it down on the table in front of me.

‘Rachel, this is for you.’

‘What is it?’ I asked, adjusting my eyes to the small print.

‘It’s about a scholarship to study horticulture.’

‘Horticulture?’

I hadn’t even heard of the word. However, I was intrigued when I found out its meaning. It turned out that grants were available to suitable applicants to assist them to train for a career in horticulture at a college known as An Grianán in Termonfeckin, County Louth. It seemed there were jobs available for young women in this field, especially in planting and taking cuttings in greenhouses and nurseries. I was really excited by the prospect despite the reservations of other colleagues, who pointed out that college places were generally reserved for the children of big farmers. Ignoring their reservations, I applied.

At my interview for the college, I was able to impress with my knowledge of the benefits of winter cabbage and the different varieties of apples. All of this knowledge had been acquired from Dad over the years in which I had helped him in his garden. I had a sense even then that I could follow in his footsteps.

In the days after my interview, I felt like a child waiting for Christmas as I kept an eye out for what I hoped would be a letter of acceptance from the interview board. The days slipped by and I began to give up hope. A little later, having got no response and because it was school holidays, I went to stay with my cousin, the late Kathy Hoare, in Coventry, England. Kathy was a district nurse and an energetic woman who looked after young emigrants from Ireland and helped them to get jobs and accommodation. I worked as a waitress and, thanks to Kathy's encouragement and help, I applied to attend college in Rugby to train as a teacher. I was accepted by the teacher training college but, in the same week that I received the offer, I received a letter from An Grianán. It was offering me a place to study horticulture in Ireland. There was no question but that I was going home.

And so it was that on a bright September morning in 1974, at the ripe old age of 22, I started out on the convoluted journey from Clonmore to my new campus near the sea in County Louth. It would involve getting a bus from Hacketstown to Dublin, a train from Dublin to Drogheda and a taxi to the campus. It was the beginning of a new life.

Rachel's Reflection

What I perceived as an error of subject choice at second level was actually a great bonus for the unseen future that lay ahead. What would I now tell my 18-year-old self?

ROOTS

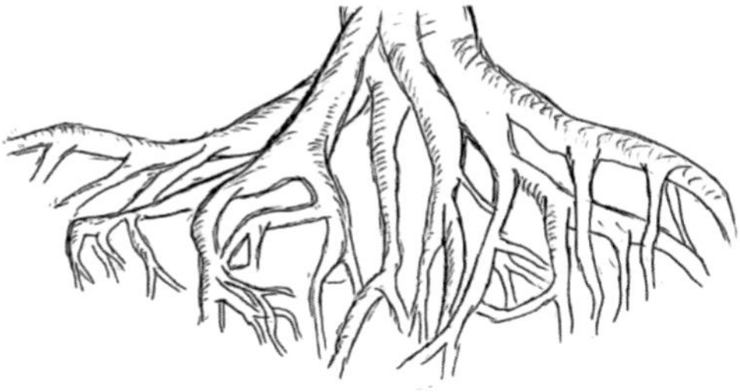

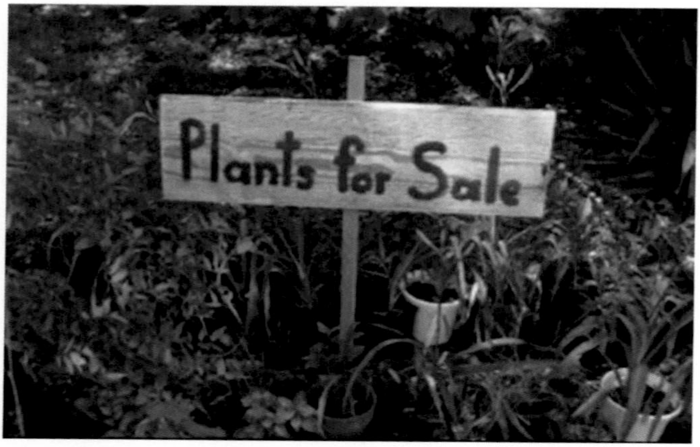

My very basic first sign

Pat, John, Jimmy, Nancy and Rachel

Dad and Mam with cup for best garden

The bungalow – where it all began

Tractor sowing potatoes, Rachel on left

Dad on the porch

First-class Honours

Hazel (*Corylus avellana*)

The Celts associated this tree with wisdom and poetic inspiration. It was believed that the edible nuts had magic power.

When my taxi turned into the grounds of the horticultural college, I was in awe – in awe of the long avenue of lime trees, in awe of the historic building and in awe of the location, which was just a short walk from the coast. I decided instantly that I would love the place, and I did. Despite some initial homesickness, I settled in very quickly. I was 22 years of age, a mature student in an age when that was not the norm. I was studious and determined to learn all I could about the science of horticulture. So, it was just as well that I had an aptitude for it.

My course was in commercial horticulture, and this involved studies in plant science, climatology, meteorology, work study, time management, crop culture, machinery, amenity horticulture, garden design, buildings and glasshouse technology, marketing, soil structure and nursery production. It goes without saying that it also required intensive knowledge of plants of all kinds. The courses were constructed so that we spent half the day in the classroom and the other half at practical work – either in the walled garden, the glasshouses with the ornamental plants or the field section where all the fruit and vegetables were grown.

In Termonfeckin we had seven acres of carrots, which were hand-harvested by the students, with varying degrees of enthusiasm. Occasionally a girl would come down with a mystery illness when the time came to pick the carrots. We called it 'carrotitis' among ourselves. There were also several acres of brassicas and other vegetables, including asparagus, which I saw here for the first time in my life. The extensive glasshouses were used to grow crops that needed winter protection, such as tomatoes, cucumbers, aubergines, peppers and strawberries. Also in the glasshouses were poinsettias, which were grown for the Christmas market. Poinsettia was another plant that was new to me. It was not seen at Christmastime in Clonmore! The Pleasure Garden, where the trees and shrubs were grown, was not only for admiring trees but also for practical work. Here the concepts of design and planning were apparent. We learned about amenity horticulture, which covers design, planning and the maintenance of plants, and then commercial horticulture, which covers fruit and vegetables.

We supplied fruit and vegetables to the Dublin City Fruit and Vegetable Wholesale Market, which was in Smithfield. At that market we were exposed to the practice of buying and selling the produce. This was my first real taste of commercial horticulture in action. The market was fun and we always enjoyed the journeys to it. On one occasion, when I was in the market at six in the morning, I received my first proposal of marriage. The proposer was quite taken with my buying and selling ability!

We got a good grounding on plant identification from Miss Rosemary McVittery, one of our lecturers. Every Wednesday afternoon, we would have to identify thirty different specimens. These would be laid out on a long table in a room and would consist of seeds, weeds, shrubs, and trees. Miss McVittery could get quite cross if we failed to identify each of them.

At an examination in our final year, one of our lecturers, Mr Billy Cummins, had laid out several specimens for us to identify. Among them was a strange black seed, round on one side and flat on the other. I remembered I had seen it somewhere in the past and had noted its unusual shape. 'Asparagus' popped into my head so I put it down on my exam paper. At the 'postmortem' after the exam, Mr Cummins was amazed that I had got it right. It had flummoxed the rest of the class.

Perhaps because I was a mature student, I was made head girl and was much trusted by the college authorities. I don't think they would have approved of my leading a group out through the windows of our residence one evening to go to a Thin Lizzy concert. We all wanted to see and hear Phil Lynott. My sons can hardly believe that their goody-goody mother would have done such a thing. I am not sure why I told them this story in the first place. Rest in peace, Phil.

I am still friends with many of my fellow students. One of those friends, Julie Murphy, nee Mackey, from Nenagh, used to have the use of her father's car, a Triumph Toledo, and this greatly added to our enjoyment. She was the only one of us who could drive at the time. We continue to meet from time to time and love to share memories of our college days, a time of innocent enjoyment and deep learning.

I often reflect on the way we were trained in college at Termonfeckin: one half of the day in the classroom and the other half out in the grounds. As well as learning about plants and the science of horticulture, we were trained in the practical side of gardening. We were taught how to double dig, take a cutting, identify a plant, and design and plant up a border. Now in Arboretum we sometimes find ourselves interviewing horticulture graduates who don't know a daisy from a dandelion. They look askance when asked about the benefits or disadvantages of double digging. They seem to have missed out on the practical side of horticulture. This, in my opinion, is a great pity. At our interviews for horticulturists, we now set out twenty common plants and ask the interviewees to identify as many as they can. If they fail to identify ten out of the twenty, we terminate the interview. We have met some interviewees who couldn't identify laurel, lavender, hydrangea in flower, roses in flower, pansies and primulas. Learning about plants and their provenance is a very necessary part of a gardening course. However, I think it is a pity that this aspect of horticulture is not combined with the practical side of growing plants.

Because it was so difficult and costly to go home to Clonmore by public transport, I didn't get home often and was happy to spend most of my free time at the college. Frequently at weekends, I would go down to the beach that adjoins the college with my friend Kathleen Carroll, née Whelan, from Wexford. Boyfriends were not our favourite topic of conversation when we were first immersed in life in Termonfeckin; would you believe we would discuss peas, beans, brassicas, fruit trees and the like?

I loved every minute of my two years in Termonfeckin. When I qualified with a first-class honours diploma, I can say, hand on heart, that it wasn't because I was a brilliant student but because I had a purpose. I could never acquire enough knowledge on my chosen subjects. I am still learning and feel it would take me several lifetimes to get all the information I want about plants.

Rachel's Reflection

Happiness lies ... in the joy of achievement, in the thrill of creative effort.

Franklin D. Roosevelt

Handsome Young Man

The Wedding Cake Tree

(*Cornus controversa 'Variegata'*)

This tree is said to represent love and passion.

The flowers are closely connected to Christianity and symbolise rebirth.

There must have been something in the air. Coming up to St Valentine's Day, six months into my course in Termonfeckin, I decided to make my first trip home. I passed the time on the bus by trying to identify all the trees and shrubs I spotted along the way. After a long-awaited reunion with my parents, I met up with some friends and they twisted my arm into going to dance in Tullow, which was roughly ten miles away. There I got chatting to a man a few years older than me, a certain Frank Doyle. I knew him vaguely because he used to drop into McCall's shop on occasion to buy cigarettes.

As our conversation continued, I discovered he had been in America, where he had done reasonably well for himself, but had returned because of the untimely death of his father in a road accident. He told me all about his life, including his job in Dublin as a salesman. At the end of the night, we said our goodbyes. Although I had enjoyed our chat, I still hadn't boyfriends on my mind.

The following weekend Frank called out to my home in Clonmore hoping that I might be there. However, I had returned to college in Termonfeckin. Mam and Dad were very impressed by this handsome young man and, perhaps because of the disappointed look on his face, invited him in for tea. I was not best pleased when I heard about it, but Frank persisted and we soon began to go out together. Now I came home more regularly and Frank would drive me back to Termonfeckin on Sunday evenings. From then on, the chats with my friend Kathleen were no longer all about plants!

At the beginning of our courtship, I wasn't really interested in a steady relationship, not least because of my budding career plans, but I gradually changed my mind. Frank and I got on very well together. I came to respect him and looked forward to our time together. I gradually realised that he was fun to be with, and he was kind and generous.

Frank and I used to meet in Dublin on the way home for the weekend and occasionally he would take me to the National Boxing Stadium. It is a measure of how much I cared for him at that stage that it took a long time before I told him that I hated boxing. However, horse-racing was somewhat different. Racing is a vibrant industry in the Carlow area. After the Curragh in Kildare, the area boasts the highest bloodstock activity in the country. Frank's father worked with horses, and Frank has always had a great interest in racing as a result. In his company, I have attended all the great racecourses around the world – Ascot and

Cheltenham in England, Happy Valley in Hong Kong, Churchill Downs in the US, Meydan in Dubai, and Caulfield in Australia – and, of course, all the racecourses in Ireland. While I'm still not the most enthusiastic racegoer in the world, I think racing certainly beats boxing. Unlike Frank, who will follow any form of sporting endeavour, I am immune to the charms of almost all sports.

After a few months Frank asked me to marry him. I said yes, putting any thoughts he might have had of returning to America out of his head. Although I hadn't marriage on my mind at all, I didn't see it as something that would get in the way of any career plans I might hatch. It is said that opposites attract, and that is certainly true of Frank and me. We are two very different individuals. I am the dreamer and he is the practical one. Often when I have one of my creative ideas, Frank's response is, 'There's no harm dreaming.'

However, when I set out to pursue my dreams, which I usually do, he is always supportive.

From the earliest days of our courtship, Frank got on very well with my parents and the rest of my family. My family has always been the centre of my life, and it was very important for me that Frank was so acceptable to them. He is a wonderful man, my best friend and soulmate. It takes a strong relationship to survive working every day with someone, and Frank and I have stood the test of time on that score.

We were married in the lovely little church of Our Lady of the Wayside in my native village on 7 August 1976 and the wedding reception was held in the beautiful village of Woodenbridge in the Vale of Avoca, County Wicklow. It was a wonderful day but it was over so quickly. Perhaps that is how most people remember their wedding day. We had no money to spend on an expensive wedding and there was no question of borrowing any. Thanks to Mam's example and tuition in sewing and baking, however, I was able to save money by making my own wedding dress and baking my own cake.

I made the wedding dress out of white satin and lined it with regular lining fabric and tulle. I made blue silk dresses for my two bridesmaids, namely Bridie Candy, who was my sister-in-law, and Frank's sister Ann. I had wanted my sister Nancy to be a bridesmaid but she had announced she was pregnant and was due soon after the wedding. I baked a four-tier wedding cake and had ambitious plans to decorate it with raised trellis corners of icing. Each intricate trellis piece was piped onto a greased stainless steel cream hornet gadget and, after a few days, when it was properly set, I heated it slightly so I could slide it off prior to attaching it to each corner of the cake. I put the pieces of trellising on chairs in our little-used parlour so they would have time to set completely before being attached to the cake. While they were setting we had unexpected visitors –

important visitors who couldn't be entertained in our kitchen as most would – and Dad directed them into the parlour while Mam busied herself making the tea in the kitchen. He was in such a flap that he sat on one of the chairs without noticing the icing trellises on it and my works of art were destroyed. My lovely Dad was hugely embarrassed because he knew that I'd spent many hours making this intricate icing and would have to do it all over again. However, I couldn't stay cross with him for long.

I have a flair for arranging flowers and while in college did a course in floristry. We learned the art of making wedding bouquets, so for my own wedding I was able to make all the floral arrangements for myself and my bridesmaids. Also, with the help of my sister-in-law Patty, I decorated the church where the wedding was to take place. For this, we used all the flowers from Dad's garden. Flower arranging is a skill that I continue to practise for the weddings of family and friends.

When my eldest son, Fergal, married Kim in her native Scotland, I was delighted to be asked by them to decorate the church and make the wedding cake. When our second son, Barry, married Lynda, I was again invited to make the bouquets, decorate the church and make the cake. These are precious memories for me.

Frank and I spent our honeymoon in Tenerife. It was the first time that I had travelled so far from home to the sun. It awoke in me an interest in travel that still persists, but it was only later, having raised my family and grown my business, that I was able to indulge this passion further. It was a passion that would eventually see me doing everything from skiing with my whole family in New Zealand to watching the setting sun paint the dizzying walls of the Grand Canyon the deepest orange, wondering how anyone who sees such things could not believe in a God; but, for now, all this would have to be put on hold.

Our first home after our wedding was a four-bedroom bungalow on half an acre that Frank had built just outside the village of Leighlinbridge, nearly an hour by car from Clonmore. It is a beautiful village and I was immediately taken by its narrow, winding streets, old buildings, ruined Norman castle and 14th-century bridge over the River Barrow. The bridge, known locally as the Valerian Bridge because of the valerian growing all over it, is considered to be the oldest working bridge in Europe. The fact that it is known as the 'garden village' endeared it to me all the more. I felt it was the kind of place where a young woman could make plans.

Rachel's Reflection

Little do you realise when you first meet someone special that this might be the most important person in your life to help guide, shape and share your dreams and walk your walk.

Plants for Sale

Beech (*Fagus sylvatica*)

In Celtic mythology the beech was thought to have medicinal properties. It is also associated with knowledge and wisdom.

Life has a way of giving you dreams to follow if you are willing to pursue them. When my dream of going to college had been realised, another had immediately taken its place: I was determined to open a garden centre. As a newlywed, I had been getting some work as a substitute teacher but I felt teaching was no substitution for working with plants, which was my passion. Although teaching gave me free time after three o'clock in the afternoon to sow plants, I simply didn't have the money to do what I envisaged. To overcome this, I decided I would need to work at anything I could to put enough funds together. Over the following years, I would do exactly that. The plan was to buy stock and operate the business from home. I never saw it as a mere hobby; it was to be profitable from the get-go. Indeed, I saw it as my future – and, as luck would have it, there was no other garden centre around.

‘Of course people want plants,’ I told my new husband and family as they questioned me on my big dream.

I knew from the beginning that my new enterprise was to be called Arboretum. This name is usually given to collections of trees in botanical gardens but I thought it would be appropriate for my new concern. I have a love affair with trees and I devoted much of my time in my student days to learning their names and recognising every variety I came across.

I laid out my garden centre in my half-acre plot with the help of Dad, Frank and my brothers. Based on a plan I had drawn up, we made very simple beds with oak railway sleepers, which we laid out in a way that we thought would allow the customer to see everything. I hadn't heard of customer-flow management at the time but had an intuitive sense of its importance. Soon after laying out the beds, Frank and I purchased a greenhouse. When erecting it, my Dad and brothers arrived to offer help once more. I was delighted with the purchase, which cost us £500, but it wasn't in place long when a helpful friend using a digger to shift a large amount of stones accidentally reversed into it and flattened it. I was distraught. It was the first of many setbacks. As with all the setbacks, however, I learned a lot from the experience.

The suppliers of the greenhouse, Lenehans of Capel Street in Dublin, were more than helpful when we went back to them all forlorn following our misfortune. I have never forgotten their help with sorting out replacement stanchions and horticultural glass at a really good price. It was an example of excellent customer service. I sent many people to their shop for years afterwards. I loved my greenhouse. I couldn't count the number of cuttings that were rooted in it or the number of seeds sown, germinated and potted in it.

My lovely greenhouse would be involved in another mishap some years later. In 1982, when my first son, Fergal, was a young boy, he came rushing into the greenhouse to tell me something important, fell through the glass and cut his hands. Our housekeeper, Noeleen, and a nurse who lived next door, Kitty, came to the rescue, and it all ended well with bandaged hands and loads of ice cream.

When I had built up a supply of plants to sell, the up-and-over garage door of the garage served as my shop window. We bought in hedging and a limited supply of garden sundries. Our opening hours were from half three on weekday afternoons, when I got home from school, and all day on Saturday and Sunday. I placed an advertisement in the local newspaper, *The Nationalist and Leinster Times*, erected a crudely painted sign stating 'Plants for sale' on a timber plank and waited for my first customer.

Frank and I applied to join the farm modernisation scheme for a grant to erect a polytunnel, only to discover that we didn't qualify because we owned less than two acres. When we were eventually able to purchase a field across the road and thereby become eligible, we found that the grant had been abolished. However, we were determined that, come hell or high water, we would get our tunnel built. I learned early on in my career that there would be many bumps in the road. Frank and I resolved that the best way to deal with setbacks was to depend on each other, our family and friends and carry on with what we were doing.

One task that was always going to involve a bump in the road was getting a loan from a bank. The difficulty in those days was that banks did not take a woman seriously, so when I was looking for my first loan I had to take Frank with me. It was such nonsense. The application process was exceptionally tough. We were looking for only £2,000 at the time, which was not the earth, but we were made jump through hoops. Some banks refused to hear my proposals at all. It was a bank in Tullow that eventually loaned me what I needed.

I continued to teach at this time and supplemented my income by giving evening classes in gardening in Bagenalstown and Carlow vocational schools. This terrified me. I was particularly intimidated by the fact that there was a lecturer from a local institute of technology in one of my classes. To make things worse, he often arrived late, which used to throw me off course every time. However, he later became a really good friend. He had such a love of gardening.

Primary school teaching helped me a little in dealing with my fear, but only a little. It is one thing teaching children in first class and quite another teaching adults, especially if you think they are highly intellectual. I used to have the most awful butterflies in my stomach on the way to classes. I used to say to myself that if they all marched the one way, I would be OK. I helped them march the same way by being totally prepared. I'm a firm believer in the maxim that by failing to prepare, you are preparing to fail. Another technique I had was to take a deep breath and count to six before opening my mouth in front of a classroom of expectant faces.

Although I never fully got rid of my fear, I learned to control it. And soon I was giving talks anywhere I was invited to give one. Although I was paid for some of this work, I was not paid for it all, but I needed to do as much of it as I could to get my name out there. I was exceptionally busy as there was no one else doing the sort of thing I was doing. To add to the pressure, I was also designing gardens. I have lost count of how many. Today, while driving around my area, I see now-mature gardens that I designed and tall, healthy trees I planted as cuttings. The hard graft I had to put in to get my business up and running gives me a great sense of pride. In the early days, it was not unusual for us to get up at four o'clock on a Saturday morning to do work on a garden and then come home to open the garden centre for nine. It was crazy stuff, but this was what it took to fulfil my dream. In fairness to Frank, he always went along with it. He was my rock and I couldn't have succeeded without him.

I must have been making a name for myself thanks to my gardening classes in Bagenalstown and Carlow because the editor of *The Nationalist and Leinster Times*, the late Liam Bergin, called out to our house to ask me to write a weekly gardening column for the paper. I wasn't home but Frank was, and he accepted the offer on my behalf. Perhaps it was just as well that I wasn't there to hear the proposal because I wouldn't have had the confidence in myself or my writing to agree to do it. I wrote this column for sixteen years. It was published with a head-and-shoulders photograph and it gave me publicity and credibility in the gardening world, not least as a woman. I was then invited to write a weekly gardening column for the national newspaper the *Sunday Independent*, which I would do for many years. I also wrote articles for other publications such as *Garden Heaven*, *Woman's Way* and *The Irish Garden*. All of this helped with the business. As I got busier, I depended on my Dad and brothers, a good friend from college days, Kathleen Carroll, and my brother Pat's wife, Patty Candy, for help with the seeds, plants and cuttings.

Our social life in those days revolved around visiting friends and family in their homes. Michael and Anne Buggie have been among our best friends for over forty years and we used to meet frequently, usually in each other's homes. Their three girls were around the same age as our boys and they all got on well. Anne and I love cooking, so our families would meet on Sunday evenings for good food and chat. Every Easter we used to attend a Mass celebrated at a ‘Mass rock’ in Oughaval Wood in Stradbally, near Anne and Michael’s home. We attended this for many years. I love the memories it evokes. Michael and Anne have been part of our lives for so long and we value their friendship.

My efforts to balance my social life and business meant there was never a dull moment. Travel was becoming a necessary part of running my enterprise and often took up considerable time. I remember having to drive all the way to Mellifont Abbey in County Louth with my sister-in-law Patty to purchase ‘liners’, small rooted cuttings of plants, and the usual seedlings of bedding plants. All these cuttings had to be potted and grown on in the tunnel that we had built on our newly acquired extra land.

A particularly successful cash crop for us was the Lombardy poplar (*Populus nigra*). Poplars are known as the ‘trees of the people’. The Lombardy poplar was a tree much used for shelterbelts and the biomass project in the 1970s thanks to research done by the Teagasc organisation in Oak Park in Carlow. It was also easy to produce. A nine-inch hardwood cutting inserted into the ground through black plastic sheeting that I had spread over a section of the garden would produce a young sapling seven to eight feet in height in six or seven months. They sold well at the time and added considerably to the profitability of our business. I feel nostalgic when I see that all these trees have now grown into fine specimens. I remember so well taking them as cuttings years ago.

We put in another tunnel at the bottom of our newly acquired field and I decided to grow chrysanthemums, as we had done when I was at college. I bought in rooted cuttings from the Princess Anne range. The perfectly formed blooms were incurved, which means were in true sphere form, and had a great range of colours, from cream and bright yellow to purple and pink. We grew them through sheepwire that was moved up on canes as the plants grew. This method kept the stems straight and strong. The plants looked good and were in bloom as we were getting them ready for the Dublin flower market. But then disaster struck. We hadn't realised there was a frost pocket at the end of the field where we had placed our tunnel. One night we had a bad frost and the beautiful chrysanthemum flowers fell off their stems as I touched them. It was a very important lesson learned the hard way. The boxes I had bought for the chrysanthemums were never used. I never grew them again.

We used tunnelling to house the thousands of bedding plants that we had for sale. Fruit trees were popular at the time and we grew all varieties in our nursery. With Dad's help I budded thousands of roses in his garden in Clonmore and succeeded in growing them on and selling them. As I have said, I never had an idle moment, but life was exciting and I was fulfilling my dreams.

I learned much in those years and got used to the little instances of sexism that were probably a product of the times we lived in. It was a male-dominated world and visitors and potential buyers would frequently ask 'to see the man of the house' when they arrived. I remember well an exchange I had with one such buyer, who was looking for apple trees that would work well together.

'Is himself about?' he asked, looking over my shoulder.

'Himself would be no good to you,' I said, 'but I promise you I'll give you two varieties that will pollinate each other.'

I did just that, and he changed his tune.

I experienced the opposite side of this kind of sexism, however, when I was over nine months pregnant with my first child, Fergal. Two council employees who had come to collect some bare-rooted rowan (*Sorbus aucuparia*) saplings stood idly by and watched as I slowly dug them up and prepared them for transport. If they had had shovels, they would have been leaning on them. Two hours later I went into labour, and many hours later Fergal made his entry into the world. It was 3 February 1979.

Frank continued with his sales day job and helped out in the evenings and at weekends. We had discussed many times whether he should resign from his good, pensionable job with its company car and join me full-time in our new endeavour. Since my son Fergal had just been born, I was understandably hesitant, especially as Frank's sales figures were the second highest of his team. Besides, neither of us was immune to the bleak economic predictions we were hearing about on the news – stories of oil shocks and major industrial unrest. I pleaded with him to stay on for another six months. He was concerned that what I was doing was simply too much for one person and felt I would burn out in the longer term. He was right.

The day Frank came home and told me he had handed in his notice, I put my head in my hands and started to cry. 'Oh my God, this has to work now; this really has to work,' I said to him through my tears. However, my panic was short-lived because, literally half an hour later, I was standing up tall telling myself, 'I am going to make this work. It is going to work.' It was another big decision for both of us and an exciting prospect for me; however, determined as I was, I could not shake off my worries entirely. We now had to support two of us and a small baby and the future was likely to be uncertain. However, I am blessed with a confident outlook on life and Frank was uncomplaining and always supportive. We were young and the world of new business was our oyster.

***

Out of the blue in 1980, a momentous event occurred –

something that was to bring the greatest sorrow to my until-then-serene life. On 27 June, when doing up the roll book for the last day of the term in the school in which I was teaching, I looked through the window and spotted my two sisters-in-law Mary and Bridie pulling up in a car. When they came inside and approached me, I knew from their faces that there was something seriously wrong.

'Is it Mam or Dad?' I asked.

'It's your dad,' one of them responded. 'He's had a bit of a turn.'

They did not tell me until later, when I had arrived in Clonmore, that he'd had a heart attack and hadn't survived. He was only sixty-seven years old. His death was a terrible blow to me. It was the beginning of the most difficult time in my life.

As will now be clear, my father was my idol. He was a poet, singer, stepdancer, gardener, card player, hard worker and good provider for his family. He loved life

TRUNK

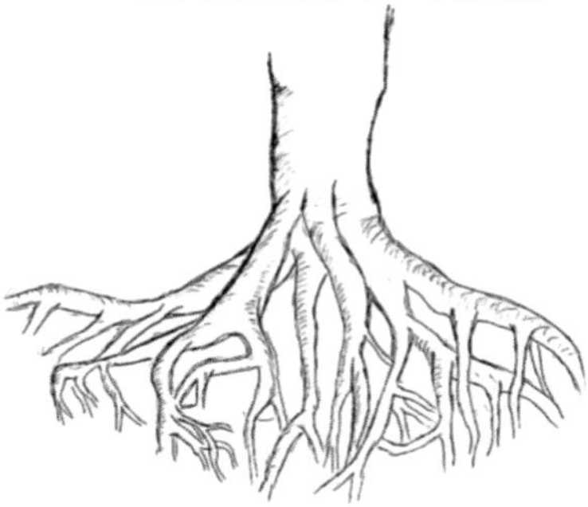

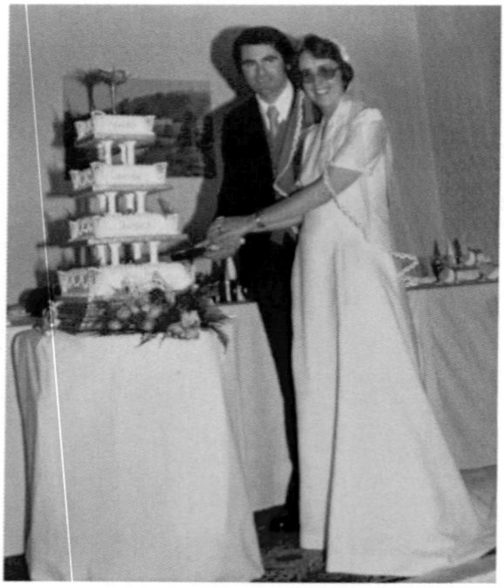

Our wedding and the cake

On our honeymoon

The Grand Canyon

Termonfeckin class on a trip to Amsterdam

Kathleen Carroll and Rachel, college friends

Frank and his sister Margaret Waites R.I.P. visiting UK garden centres in the early days

A Family Affair

The Monkey Puzzle Tree *(Araucaria araucana)*
This tree represents adventure, creativity and energy. It is an unusual conifer; its branches are covered in spirals of tough, spiny, leaflike scales. It is a native of Chile and Argentina.

The cliché that the success of any business is all about 'location, location, location' is true, or at least it was of my situation. We were living and trading just outside Leighlinbridge, a quiet, albeit beautiful, backwater, and all our customers had to travel miles from the main road to find me, many of them coming long distances. Besides, our home was not really the best place from which to run a business. Frank and I decided we should move closer to our customers, so we were pleased when, in 1982, we found a large yard to rent in the town of Carlow. Our hope was that this premises would make it easier for our customers to get to us. We were acutely conscious, however, of the barrage of news stories on the bleak economic outlook, political instability, emigration and rising debt.

In our rented yard we built a small shed to use as a shop and kept it well stocked with the full range of products needed for growing plants. We also sold tools, trellising, compost, seed trays, seeds, chemicals and fertilisers. I had stopped teaching at this stage and, although I still continued with the gardening classes and writing a weekly article for *The Nationalist and Leinster Times*, I was now concentrating full-time on the gardening business. Frank and I were also doing landscaping work. This usually meant meeting clients in the evenings when the garden centre closed and starting on the projects early in the morning before opening. We were working long hours and were beginning to succeed. We had, from our earlier efforts, built up a loyal customer base, and those customers have kept faith with us right up to the present time. Many of them have become true friends.

On 24 October 1982, our second son, Barry John, was born. Frank and I were still working long hours landscaping and in the garden centre, and the best way to proceed was of course weighing on our minds. There was no question of me not working in those early days of motherhood. Two days after Barry was born, I was back in action in the plant nursery. This didn't go unnoticed, however. My lovely neighbour Kitty, the nurse, marched over to bring me back to my senses.

'Did you or did you not give birth two days ago?' she asked.

'Yes, Kitty,' I answered.

'Then go back into the house and mind yourself.'

After that I came up with a solution. Because Kitty worked nights, she was often in bed during the day, so I used to check that her curtains were closed before heading outside. It worked, or else Kitty knew she was fighting a losing battle.

The thing is, I actually took motherhood totally in my stride. I recall that when I had been pregnant, Liam Bergin, the editor of *The Nationalist and Leinster Times*, saw fit to remind me that pregnancy was not an illness. I took his words to heart and told myself pregnancy was the most natural thing in the world. When I had no childminder and needed to work in the plant nursery, which was at our home, I would put the pram in the shade of a tree, do what I had to do, and take the baby inside when he needed feeding. Likewise, I had a Moses basket for the children in the car if I had no option but to take them with me on a journey. They never interrupted my work and I never saw them as getting in the way of it. That was the way at the time.

Having said all that, Frank and I were lucky that we always had the most wonderful childminders. My sister-in-law Patty and her husband, my brother Pat, were happy to bring our boys to their own home when required. Our neighbours, the late Breda and Jim Aylward were always willing to help, as was my sister Nancy and her husband Richie Kavanagh. We were happy that our boys were in good hands when we could not be with them.

While our extended family helped us with childminding, we were especially fortunate when a young woman from Leighlinbridge, Noeleen Doyle, joined our team to help mind our sons. Yes, she is the very same Noeleen who came to our rescue when Fergal had the collision with a glass pane in our greenhouse. She had just completed her leaving certificate. Ever since she joined us, she has looked after my whole family in countless ways. Ten years ago she undertook the minding of the next generation of the Doyle family. She used to divide her week between minding Fergal and Kim's two girls, Blair and Bébhinn, and Barry and Lynda's three boys, Frankie, Evan and Liam, while still looking after Frank and myself. Noeleen has now decided to care for her own family but will always be an important part of ours. She received a special honour for her long and loyal service at our annual staff awards ceremony. It was presented to her by Frank, Fergal, Barry and me in the company of our guest speaker, Davy Fitzgerald, who hurled for Clare and trained the Wexford hurling team, and in the presence of our own team. We are delighted that Noeleen pays regular visits to our families and to the Arboretum.

While Frank and I concentrated on our landscaping business in the early 1980s, we employed a young horticulturist, our neighbour's daughter, Catherine Aylward, to work in the garden centre in Carlow town. We were still growing plants under plastic and outside in Leighlinbridge. Although business was good in the garden centre, it was difficult to make a profit. It was a time of rising unemployment and cutbacks, and customers were understandably cautious with their money. The then Taoiseach, Charles J. Haughey, had just told us all to tighten our belts. To top things off, we were paying a weekly rent of £121, which was huge. We felt this rent was dead money and that it would be best to own our own property. So, when a one-acre site in Carlow town came on the market, we decided to buy it and move once more. The site was on the banks of the Burren River and opposite the popular Superquinn store. Getting a loan was not without its problems but our application was accepted. I later learned that my brothers, Jimmy, John and Pat, had decided that if things went wrong, they would club together and bail us out if necessary. The kindness of my family was unique and heart-warming. When all was said and done, we succeeded in making the purchase.

When we moved to the River Burren site, we decided to make it a showcase for the plants we sold. We built a pergola that went right up the garden and we planted climbing roses and wisteria to cover it. This pergola was ahead of its time but, as we would find out later, it was not without its problems. We built a shop for the usual garden centre products.

Some time previously, on a trip to Nottingham to visit Margaret Waites, Frank's late sister, I had gone to the local garden centre and had seen it had a café. I was really impressed with this idea because I thought it added much value to the enterprise. Now, embarking on a new venture with a new site and new building, I saw an opportunity: I ensured our shop would be large enough to house a café. R&D, a much-used abbreviation in the business world, stands for 'research and development', but I have a different interpretation and take it to mean 'rob and duplicate'. Ideas are free and there is no copyright on them. A popular song sung by Finbar Furey at the time was called 'Red Rose Café' and we thought that was an appropriate name for our new venture. Our café was the first in a garden centre in Ireland, and it was the centre of attention when broadcaster and garden writer Gerry Daly opened our new Arboretum on 26 October 1985.

To say this was a busy time in my life would be a gross understatement. Frank and I were now employing five people, continuing to operate our landscaping business, running a plant nursery at our home in Leighlinbridge and rearing two small sons. On top of all that, I was doing most of the cooking for the café. I used to get up at four o'clock in the morning to bake cakes, scones, rock buns, coconut buns and pastries. There were just not enough hours in the day for all the work we had to do and to find time to devote to two small boys. Frank, in particular, was concerned that I was doing too much, so, with great reluctance, we made a decision to franchise out the café. It gave me more time to spend with Frank and our boys and to run the rest of the business, but I missed the involvement with the food and the human interaction that came from providing good wholesome fare to appreciative customers.

Business in our new site was good and we soon earned a reputation far beyond our immediate surroundings. Visitors came from as far away as Cork and Dublin and word got around that there was a special garden centre in Carlow. We had a 'Connoisseurs' Corner' for rare plants, which was especially popular. It was here that I first met Carmel Duignan, who has now become a firm friend. She is a keen gardener, gardening writer and lecturer. She has a great love of the rare and exotic in plants. It was fitting that we should meet in the Connoisseurs' Corner. Around the same time, I met well-known gardener and television presenter Dermot O'Neill, who remained a close friend until his death in 2022. Diarmuid Gavin, celebrity gardener, and Gerry Daly, the father of gardening in Ireland, are friends of Arboretum as well as being personal friends.

In the garden centre we had wisterias on frames, magnolias of all kinds, *Ligustrum* topiary and mature *Ginkgo biloba* trees. I particularly remember purchasing a consignment of maples – *Acer japonicum* cultivars – and magnolias from Italy. These were beautiful small trees and shrubs. When they first arrived, I used to go out frequently just to admire them. They were hardly in place when Jim Bolger, a friend, famous horse trainer and lover of trees and plants, arrived and said, 'I want to buy the lot.' Although his offer was very welcome because the plants were not cheap and could have been difficult to sell, I was reluctant to see them go. However, pragmatism conquered sentiment and the sale was made.

By necessity, our two boys spent a lot of their time with us in the garden centre. Noeleen used to bring them in practically every day, and when they started school they spent almost all of their free time with us. It is very gratifying to Frank and me that this early immersion in the enterprise did not turn them away from the horticulture industry. I recall a conversation with Frank in which I said they would either hate it all or grow to love it. Where Barry was concerned, it turned out I had little to fear. In those days, I used to make weekly trips to Kilkenny and I'd take Barry with me one week and Fergal the next, and both of them on the third week. I had discovered that bringing them one at a time was the only way to find out how they were getting on in school. One afternoon when it was Barry's turn to accompany me, he looked out the car window when we were passing through the small village of Royal Oak and said, 'Look at that *Clematis montana* "Rubens"! Isn't it fabulous?' I was so stunned that I nearly drove over the ditch. Fergal, on the other hand, was not enthusiastic about horticulture but would eventually find his own path.

Having two small boys spend so much time in their mother's workplace might not have turned out so well, however. On a now-famous occasion when Barry was a toddler, he went missing in the garden centre and couldn't be found anywhere. Everyone on the premises and beyond was involved in the search. My consternation grew by the second and I was almost sick with the thought that he might have fallen into the river that flowed at the bottom of our site. Having said that, I could find no gaps in the fence that he might have slipped out through. Eventually, he was found, sound asleep in the closed boot of our Toyota Camry in the car park. He had decided he was tired, climbed into the boot and closed the lid for a snooze, totally oblivious to the panic he had caused. He was always the kind of child who would just lie down and go to sleep whenever he was tired. I can say with some certainty that my second son does not suffer from claustrophobia.

We had been aware of a fall-off in business during the winter months over the preceding three years, but especially in December, which was the worst trading month of the year. Gardening is, of course, a seasonal business and there is a natural fall-off in winter. We did not want to have to let staff go, but there was a possible solution. When abroad, we had seen Christmas displays in garden centres, so in 1990 Frank and I decided that we would 'do' Christmas. In January 1991 I set off for Harrogate in England to a trade fair with 2,000 punts – the old Irish pound – in my pocket and an idea about a theme for our Christmas display the following December. My idea was that we should feature the New Testament of the Bible, with particular emphasis on the miracles of Jesus. We had many discussions about how to do this and how we could tastefully associate a miracle with a product – a pleasing association of God and Mammon, if such is possible. During one of our planning sessions about appropriate themes, Barry, who was about nine years old at the time, suggested that we cover the lectern and the wall with black cloth and place on the lectern a large Bible open at Genesis, the first book of the Old Testament. He also suggested that we have a large banner with the words 'In the beginning, there was darkness'. This is exactly what we did. We used black and silver decorations of the kind that were fashionable at the time. It is not surprising that Barry now determines the themes for the Christmas displays.

The biblical theme worked out well in more ways than one. It happened that, unknown to me, there was a recently formed Bible group in the area whose members were delighted that we were highlighting both Testaments. They spread the word. Many of their members and their families came to the display and we had a very successful Christmas. So much so that, in January, I had a much bigger budget to bring with me to Harrogate.

***

While I had miraculous successes at Arboretum in those days, I also had catastrophes, one of which you might say was biblical in proportion. One Sunday morning in 1991, after a heavy rainfall, I arrived to open up the premises with my two small boys in tow only to spot flood water, two feet deep, through the railings of the gate. I hadn't realised that work that had been done on the Barrow river had caused the Burren to swell. I put my head against the railings to take in the awful scene. Flowerpots and all sorts of rubbish were floating in a stinking, brown slurry – a mixture of river water, drain water and foul-smelling sewage. All the plants that were not elevated on raised benches looked in danger of ruin.

'Oh my God, what am I going to do?' I said.

'Ma, are you all right?' one of the boys kept repeating, tugging at my sleeve.

The boys were old enough then to see I was in shock. I'm not sure what I said to reassure them but I knew there was no point in being paralysed with fear when something had to be done.

Just then my solicitor, Frank Lanigan, was walking by and saw the stress on my face. There wasn't much time for chit-chat.

'I need help, Frank,' I said, pointing to the devastation. 'The conifers are the most important things to be got out of that flood because they won't like their roots sitting in water.'

Frank didn't hesitate. He rushed off to his house and came back with his wellingtons and a pair that belonged to his wife for me. We waded into the filth and started moving pots of plants out of harm's way. Frank, my brothers and friends soon rallied to the cause and we eventually got everything salvageable to dry ground. We piled up sandbags to stop the water getting into the shop. Damaged plants that I thought could be nursed back to health were brought to the nursery in Leighlinbridge for tender loving care. I am so grateful to everyone who helped minimise the damage.

When the stock had been rescued, we had to close our business and set to work immediately on a project to remove the slope down to the river and ensure the next flood would not inundate our property. Our insurance broker at the time assured us that our policy would cover us for the damage done, but when the assessor arrived we were told a different story. He told us our successful efforts to keep the water out of the shop building with sandbags had negated the insurance cover and that we would get no recompense. Just another road bump. We were out of business for four weeks.

Although family and friends were tremendously helpful at the time of the flood, our bank at the time most certainly was not – and not for the first time. These were different times, and dealing with banks was not easy. They were not always helpful to customers who found themselves in distress. Despite the fact that we had never failed on repayments, this counted for nought when trouble came. The bank applied a significant charge to every cheque we signed to get back up and running. I have always valued our excellent credit rating and I think integrity is important for a business to flourish. In the early nineties, interest rates in the banks were in the mid-teens. Frank and I drove to the bank and met our bank manager, and I told him how disappointed we were with how the bank was treating us.

'You've kicked us when we were down; that's what you've done to us,' I said.

We had a little contretemps at which cross words followed. In the end the bank manager apologised and reversed all the charges on the cheques we had written when we had exceeded our small overdraft limit.

Some time later I was attending a course for business owners at which the speaker offered two pieces of good advice on dealing with banks that I have adhered to ever since: (1) when you want to meet the bank manager, invite them out to your business because you then have them on your patch; and (2) always use two banks. I believe in not putting all my eggs in one basket. I also now position myself at the head of the table so as to be in control, a tactic I picked up from a very suave guy who came in once to sell us a computer system. I am glad to say Arboretum has really good working relationships with its bank managers today. After the flood we had to work hard on this – not least because we would need more money quite soon.

Rachel's Reflection

The old saying that it takes a village to rear a child was so true in our case, as is evident from the wonderful people who surrounded us as our boys grew up, literally among the plants.

Back to Our Roots

Sycamore (*Acer pseudoplatanus*)

In Celtic mythology the sycamore was consecrated to Dana, the Celtic goddess of fertility. It is tolerant of wind and air pollution and is often grown as a windbreak in exposed areas.

There are some things that you just have to do. In 1990 a house near Leighlinbridge village with five acres of land had come on the market and Frank and I bought it. It was a beautiful, three-storey nineteenth-century house in need of repair. It had no heating and there were bats hanging from the decorative cornicing on the top floor; however, I was convinced that with a lot of work, it would become my dream home.

Attached to the home, but no longer part of the property, was a ten-acre field with frontage to the main road – the then N9, the principal road linking Dublin and Waterford and giving easy access to Kilkenny. I really believed this field was meant to be ours and was determined that, one way or another, we would purchase it. Frank, always the salesman, approached its owner and, although it was not for sale at the time, he promised to let us know if he intended to sell. In due course it came on the market and we bought it. We now had a greenfield site and stables for temporary storage.

It is worth taking a few moments to talk about our new property because I devoted a lot of time to it in parallel with running the business. While the purchase was exciting, Frank and I had no idea when we wrote the cheque of the many challenges it would throw at us, especially as we had no money left to invest in it. However, as someone who is in her element when given a decorating project, I was keen to do what I could myself. As is the case with gardening, I love to be hands-on. Because Frank was fully occupied with our landscaping business, my ever-willing and helpful

problems encountered in business. It made me reflect further on what it means to be in control in an enterprise and also on brand reputation.

In the year 2000, Frank and I started to develop our ten-acre field in Leighlinbridge for the next iteration of Arboretum. We had learned from our experience of running a retail business and resolved not to repeat any mistakes we'd made. Although I was a dreamer, I was not prepared to leave things to luck. For many years I had been learning, visualising and observing, but also mapping out the new venture. Planning permissions were sought and eventually the builders started work. My idea was to design a centre like a racetrack system, not because of Frank's love of the sport of kings but because I had seen this on my travels and considered it to be an excellent way to promote good customer flow. My vision was that the customers would enter the shop amid plants, follow a circular route that would allow them to see everything on display, and then exit through houseplants. I was all too aware that a major mistake I had made in Carlow was cutting the garden centre in two with a pergola, effectively meaning that customers who went to the left could not see what was on the right, and vice versa.

We already knew that food was a great footfall driver but now we had to persuade people that it was worth their while to drive some distance to reach us. To this end we determined that the café would be under our control and that we would have very good food that was sourced locally and cooked on the premises. We also intended the food to be organic where possible. We ran a competition and asked our customers to help us name the café. The winner, who chose the name Mulberry's Restaurant, won a weekend away. We set aside a large room for the enterprise, which was to seat sixty people, and recruited chefs and kitchen staff. We included a conference centre in the building. We had seen garden centres with conference facilities in operation on our travels and thought such facilities would be a good addition to our business. Groups of people and businesses would hold their conferences in this location, where parking was free, where excellent food was served and where we could provide all the other facilities they needed.

On 6 February 2001, together with our team of five from the Arboretum in Carlow, we moved overnight to our new premises in Leighlinbridge. We were trading in Carlow on Tuesday 6 February, and on Wednesday 7 February we opened our doors in Leighlinbridge. Our friend Jim Bolger – the horse trainer who had purchased an entire consignment of exotic trees years earlier – performed the opening ceremony on Saturday 10 March, 2001. Jim had encouraged us in moving from Carlow. At the time, this was important because many people questioned our wisdom in leaving the populous town of Carlow to run a business in the beautiful backwater that is Leighlinbridge.

I trusted my gut feeling that if I built it they would come, and I was proven right. I hope that, in realising my plans, I allowed my passion and enthusiasm to show. After all, positivity is worth its weight in gold. It is in my nature and I always believe everything is going to work out well. I recall being complimented on my positivity the night I received a Carlow County Council social responsibility award and the Carlow Person of the Year award in November 2013. John Behan, one of Fergal and Barry's teachers from Knockbeg College in Carlow, told me that I was the most positive person he had ever met. Thank you, John Behan. The social responsibility award recognises voluntary contributions to improving the quality of life in the community. I believe I got it because I had given advice to the council on many projects over the years, such as determining whether trees should be condemned, working with many voluntary groups and advising on planting in villages throughout the county. The Carlow Person of the Year was chosen from all the award-winners on the night. I was very pleased to receive both.

Rachel's Reflection

Create your own vision, work hard, continuously strive to learn more and aim for excellence.

A Little Bit of Heaven

The Birch (*Betula pendula*)
The silver birch was a symbol of renewal and purification to the ancient Celts. Samhain (what we now know as Halloween) was the start of the Celtic year. People would burn bundles of birch twigs to drive out the spirits of the old year.

A garden is so much more than a place of consolation and joy. This is particularly true of my private garden. Not long after I had moved into my beautiful old home in Leighlinbridge, my friend Carmel Duignan gave me a gift of a schleffera plant, nicknamed the umbrella tree because of how its elongated leathery leaves radiate from a central point. To me, getting a present of a plant is truly special. Sadly, my prized umbrella plant lasted only until the first hard frost, or about five years, but there was something to be learned from this. I saw an opportunity in it. I began to realise that my private garden could be used as a kind of laboratory in which to test unusual plants to see whether they would work in the Irish climate. I certainly did not want to sell to Arboretum customers plants and products that I couldn't grow myself.

The same applies to products. I frequently try out new products in my own garden first to see if they do exactly what they say on the tin. One such product was SwellGell, a granular material you add to soil to help retain moisture. The minuscule granules absorb hundreds of times their own weight in water, swelling to the point where they look like frogspawn. I was so happy with water-retaining gels that I never plant a hanging basket in spring nowadays without using them. My first trial of SwellGel was about thirty years ago in my own glasshouse. On the right-hand side I hung baskets with the granules and on the left I hung baskets without them. The ones on the right did much better. At the time of the trial, I was producing about 250 hanging baskets per year for Mackey's in Mary Street, Dublin, so the results of my experimentation proved very valuable to me. It helped me to retain my contract with Mackey's for many years.

Having learned about design in college in Termonfeckin and having designed and landscaped countless gardens with Frank, the time had come to apply my knowledge in my own garden. I wanted a garden with my own stamp on it and, it goes without saying, I wanted to put myself to the test. When designing for others, my habit had always been to walk through their houses first because I knew that they would also be looking at their gardens from the inside. A useful benefit of this was that it gave me a sense of their style and whether they would prefer a flowery garden or, like me, one filled with a wide variety of shrubs and trees, but particularly trees. Before designing my private garden, I had developed a clear sense of how I wanted it to look through the tall, narrow nineteenth-century windows of my home. The view through these windows was one of wonderful mature trees that Frank and I were lucky enough to inherit when we purchased our home: a stately beech as old as the house, dating it at 1830, and a venerable weeping silver birch (*Betula pendula*).

One of the first principles of design I wanted to try out was the incorporation of paths that veer off in different directions to reveal little surprises, such as a shrubbery, birdbath, statue or seat. Near the house, I created a lavender walk by planting over a thousand plants of lavender 'Munstead' on two sunny, well-drained banks that face each other. This creates a beautiful vision from the conservatory when the plants are in flower and buzzing with bees. Lavender is short-lived so, when my plants were fifteen years old, I replaced them with a compact, deep-purple variety called Essence Purple. This sea of purple is edged with low-growing box hedging (*Buxus sempervirens*).

Frank and I discovered an old concrete bunker in our garden shortly after we moved in. I cannot think what it was used for but it was almost two metres deep, full of water and very dangerous, especially when you have two little boys who fancy themselves as the next Ernest Shackleton. I filled it up with stones and then put down a layer of topsoil, in which I planted a 'Brown Turkey' fig tree (*Ficus carica*), the best variety for our climate. It is now thriving. Figs need to have their root-run curtailed or they will put on a lot of vegetation at the expense of producing fruit. My fig tree is in an ideal spot and I adore its beautiful lobed leaves and soft, delicious fruit. I grew another fig in a large pot for decorative effect and, one day a few years ago, I counted fifty fruits on it. This was a proud moment for me, as it would be for any horticulturist. I was delighted with my crop. Before harvesting, I wait until each fruit has a drop of sweet nectar at the bottom.

Halfway down our lavender walk is an icehouse. Icehouses were found only in big houses before the invention of refrigerators in the 1850s. Ours was effectively an underground chamber insulated with straw or sawdust. I understand that in bygone winters the River Barrow was dammed and that when it froze, ice was collected and dropped into my icehouse from the top. The straw or sawdust and the cool atmosphere would have ensured ice was available to the big house for most of the year. Even today the interior of the icehouse is always cold.

The path through the lavender walk leads to what I call Rachel's Folly – a circle of marble columns with a cupola of metal that I erected in a quiet corner shaded with conifers. I didn't tell Frank the cost. However, suspecting it was a considerable amount, he dropped into the office one day and casually asked one of the accounts staff if the invoice for it had come in. Our helpful employee promptly located it and the truth was out. I planted the shrub Mexican orange blossom (*Choisya ternate*) around this beautiful structure because I adore its wonderfully fragrant evergreen leaves and sweet-smelling white flowers. Outside the orange blossom, I have a circle of upright Irish yew. I love to sit at my tea-for-two furniture set under the cupola and contemplate. It is a peaceful and spiritual place for me.

Where the path continues I have a bed of various camelia varieties. These evergreens plants thrive here despite the high lime content in our area. Here too is *Magnolia grandiflora*, with its wonderful evergreen leaves and creamy white flowers that measure up to thirty centimetres across. On the other side of the path, I have planted cat mint (*Nepeta*), which thrives here and is much loved by our cats.

On the left of the conservatory is a large patio that overlooks a sweeping herbaceous border. This is framed with box hedging and ends at a trickling water fountain. The path through the herbaceous border has soft curves that are pleasing to the eye and make for relaxing transitions between each section and the next. I make sure there are plant groupings on both sides of the path so I don't get a lopsided effect. The desire to achieve balance, an intrinsic principle of design, has been ingrained in me by my studies.

To the right of the conservatory is one of my favourite parts of my garden – the Wisteria Walk. This is made up of six large Roman columns with a timber trellis attached that is completely covered with wisteria. When in flower, the scent is carried through the garden and even permeates the house when the doors are open. My favourite time of the year to look at wisteria is the early spring, when the tiny buds are just peeping out. The coronavirus pandemic gave me the time and space to really observe and enjoy that short season. Along my Wisteria Walk I have a tea-for-two set of mosaic furniture on which I can sit and contemplate the forty shades of green.

My garden is full of trees. A collection of acer varieties grow well here despite Carlow's reputation for cold winters. We also have a snake-barked maple, a Judas tree (*Cercis*), a holm oak and a beautiful tulip tree (*Liriodendron*). A great plantsman and friend, Kieran Dunne, gifted me a Princeton Gold acer (*Acer platanoides*) to celebrate my presidency of the International Garden Centre Association in 2014 and 2015. I love its bright golden foliage and stunning autumn colour. He presented me with another small maple, a Little Miss Ruby (*Acer palmatum*), spectacular with her bright red buds, to mark my appointment to the main board of Bord Bia. Thank you, Kieran. I treasure trees given to me as gifts.

The front entrance to our house is very attractive, with a set of wide stone steps leading up to an impressive 8-panel door painted cheerful yellow. More colour is added by a series of interesting urns here, always filled with beautiful foliage or topiary. Despite the inviting nature of the main entrance, the family always uses the back door. Close to the kitchen, it's in a semi-basement setting and surrounded by high walls. I designed a patio here and created a fernery in the shade provided by the walls. I have many species of ferns here – all grown in pots in the shady corner. I strategically placed mirrors of different sizes on the walls to reflect the plants and a large outdoor clock completes the 'room outside' feel of this area. On the sunny side of the patio I have several varieties of roses. They are all fragrant and my favourite is a beautiful plant with pink and peach flowers that have a wonderful perfume. It is called *Rosa* 'Rachel', so I could be accused of being prejudiced. Also grown here is the large evergreen shrub *Fatsia japonica* and two Flame of the Forest plants (*Pieris formosa 'forestii'*) in large pots. These are on either side of a large gong that was used to call the original family of the house to dinner. Opposite the door I have planted a climbing plant, a star jasmine (*Trachelospermum jasminoides)*. It grows on a frame and its flowers produce a sweet scent in summer. Nearby is another small tree, a Jacqueline Postill (*Daphne bhuloa)*, which produces scented flowers in late winter. I also have sweet box/Christmas box (*Sarcococca confusa*), which produces sweetly scented white flowers at Christmas. It's a real gem. All these plants are fragrant at different times of the year, and all are in pots and raised on what are called 'pot feet', which means I can easily move the pots around so that there is always a gorgeous fragrance as I turn the key in my door.

On each side of the door, there is a stone trough containing herbs of all sorts, which I constantly use in the kitchen. Scattered throughout this container garden is night-scented stock (*Matthiola longipetala*). This is a particular favourite because, as the common name suggests, its perfume fills the surrounding areas on summer evenings with its magic. It makes me nostalgic because it takes me back to my childhood in Clonmore, where Dad had this little plant growing everywhere. This is our *al fresco* barbeque eating area on pleasant summer days. A waterfall fountain adds another sensory element to the patio garden. There is nothing like the sound of trickling water for creating a sense of tranquillity.

I have planted a tree to mark the births of each of my grandchildren. For Blair I have a *Liriodendron tulipifera* 'Aureomarginatum' – the beautiful tulip tree with variegated leaves. This large tree is a North American native and the leaves are lobed and look as though the ends were cut off. The flowers are shaped like a tulip and are a yellow-green in colour.

Frankie's tree is a *Ginkgo biloba* 'Fastigiata', commonly known as the Maidenhair Tree. This tree is like a living fossil and is believed to be the sole surviving species of a group of trees that existed over 200 million years ago, the time of the dinosaurs. Frankie is interested in the dinosaurs, so the tree has special relevance to him as a result.

The beautiful handkerchief tree (*Davidia involucrate),* also called the dove tree or ghost tree, was planted to mark Bébhinn's birth. When it blooms in early summer, the small flowers are surrounded by white bracts that are said to resemble handkerchiefs or doves resting on the leaves. It was named after French priest Fr Armand David, who first described seeing it in China in the latter part of the nineteenth century. Father David was also the first westerner to describe the giant panda.

An American sweetgum (*Liquidamber styraciflua*) was planted to mark Evan's arrival. This deciduous tree is tolerant of most soils and, with its star-shaped, maple-like leaves, makes an attractive specimen. The sap has been used for various purposes – from making poultices to chewing gum – hence the common name. The glory of this tree is its brilliant autumn colour – leaves turn different shades of yellow and orange before they fall.

Eddie's White Wonder (*Cornus kousa*) was planted to mark the arrival of my youngest grandson, Liam. It is a small, deciduous tree that has many seasons of interest. In late spring the gleaming white flowers consist of four bracts that seem to sit on the elegant leaves. In autumn it sometimes produces inedible red, strawberry-like fruit. The leaves transform into a spectacular array of colour before they fall.

Of course, gardening is not without scourges. I have just won a long battle with a persistent and troublesome weed known as coltsfoot, or *Tussilago farfara*, whose pretty yellow flowers emerge in February and which spreads by means of rhizomes and seed. Rather than using chemicals to get rid of it, I used black polythene as a ground cover and left it in place for months. It worked. I intend to plant a new herbaceous border here.

I love my garden and the time I can spare to be in it. As the success of Arboretum bears out, I'm not alone in deriving great joy from gardening, and this makes me feel I am in the right line of business. I have experienced feelings of great tranquillity not only in my own garden but also in others I have visited all over the world. Once when I was on an International Garden Centre Association trip to Japan, I visited Kodaiji Temple in Kyoto. Such was the power of the place that when my fellow delegates and I walked into one part of its gardens, we instantly fell silent. It was dusk and all of the trees – pines, maples and tall groves of bamboo – were illuminated discreetly, conjuring up a magical reflection in a large pond. As we exited this magical area, our conversation resumed.

'This is what I expect Heaven will be like,' I said to the lady beside me, a New Zealander who has since become a really good friend.

She looked at me and became so upset that she started to cry. She informed me that her 29-year-old son, Andrew, had died only a few months previously.

'I could accept his death if he were in a place like this,' she said, looking up at the illuminated trees.

Often when sitting in my private garden, Kodaiji Temple comes to mind. My private garden is a little bit of heaven.

Rachel's Reflection

Plant a tree and you plant a future. Each tree can convert enough carbon dioxide to oxygen to sustain a family of four. With climate change in mind, it is our duty to plant more trees.

A Snake in the Roof

Larch (*Larix decidua*)

In olden times people believed that wearing a sprig of larch would protect them from enchantment and evil spirits.

One Sunday morning at three o'clock, a year into the new millennium, I received a telephone call that no mother wants to hear. It was from a doctor in the regional hospital in Cork.

'I have your son here,' he said. 'He's been in a bad accident, and I suggest you make your way to Cork to see him.'

I sat up in bed and composed myself.

'How bad? I inquired.

'He has a swelling on the brain and there's a blood vessel behind his brain leaking. We haven't cleaned him up yet as we might have to operate at any minute, so he'll look in bad shape when you come.'

I picked up a pen and notebook, which I always keep beside my bed, and asked for directions to the hospital. I wrote them down 100 percent correct. When I put down the receiver, I turned to Frank and told him what I had just heard from the doctor. He pulled the duvet over his head and didn't respond. I handed him his clothes and said, 'Put on your clothes now; we're going to Cork.' I went into Barry's room and – like father, like son – got the very same response. When he eventually sat up, he said, 'Mam, tell me I'm having a bad dream.'

On the drive to the hospital, I think I prayed the whole way, as did Barry. Frank concentrated on the road and was quiet. When we found the intensive care unit, some extremely nice doctors brought us in to see Fergal. Barry and Frank could not take it and left the room. I stood beside Fergal, held his hand and talked to him. He was able to open one of his eyes. It was only when I went out to Barry and Frank afterwards that I let the tears flow.

'Mam, I don't know how you did that. You were better than Dad and myself,' Barry said.

I held it together for Fergal. For the next week or so, I travelled up and down to Cork every day to see him. The swelling went down in his brain and surgery was not required, thank God.

Fergal had been studying business in University College Cork. After spending some time in hospital, he came home to recuperate. Fr Liam Lawton, a great friend who had taught Fergal in Knockbeg College and who subsequently became a renowned singer-songwriter, used to come to the house to sit with him. He was very good to him. I never learned what the two of them talked about but I was forever grateful to Fr Liam.

When Fergal was getting better and, probably feeling a little bored, he asked me and Frank if he could install an electronic point-of-sale system (EPOS) in the business to transform our stock management. This system, which entailed barcoding and scanning every product that we stocked, plants included, was breaking new ground in our industry at the time. We agreed to his proposition. However, we were concerned that he would do what many of his contemporaries were doing and take off to Australia or New Zealand to see some of the world before he settled down – he was only in his early twenties – so we had one proviso: that he remain for one year and train another member of the team to replace him, if necessary, so there would be no knowledge gap. He agreed to the proviso and said he wouldn't let us down. We were especially lucky at the time that he met his future wife, Kim, who was then a student at Carlow Institute of Technology. Kim was a great help to him in his recovery. He stayed on in Arboretum and trained a new recruit, my nephew Neville Candy, to use the point-of-sale system. Fergal made a complete recovery from his accident, thank God.

***

The years immediately after Fergal's crash were in the middle of the Celtic tiger years and the economy was booming. So too was Arboretum, and its 60-seat restaurant, Mulberry's, was proving to be a bigger attraction than I had foreseen. It was a good problem to have. From talking to customers, I realised that many would drop in for breakfast *en route* from Waterford and Kilkenny to Dublin. Indeed, this was recognised at the time in the hospitality guide *Georgina Campbell's Ireland*, which described the restaurant, with its pleasant ambience and wholesome, freshly prepared food, as a 'good place to break a journey'.

In addition, the lunch trade was prospering. I had become aware that people who called in for food invariably bought something else, especially those things that were close at hand, well displayed and value for money. We knew where the hot spots in the store were and we made sure to place items strategically. This is a lesson in knowing your customer. For example, we have today many regular older customers who come to Rachel's Garden Café (and Rachel's Secret Garden Café at Kilquade) twice a week. Some are on a pension and minding their pennies but there are certain things they like – resin robins at Christmas time being one – so we displayed them on the route from the front door to the café. I have to remind myself on buying trips to put myself in the shoes of our many different customer types and buy for them, not for me.

Our team had proven wrong the prophets of doom who thought that we were foolish to move from Carlow town to the countryside. So much so that within four years of our move, in 2004, builders were back on site because we wanted to expand once again to meet our growing needs. We were busier than ever before and were concerned we would not have enough parking space available. To carry out the works, we had consulted widely and had eventually chosen the late Sean Byrne, an amazing Carlow man, to draw up the plans. His plans matched exactly the vision we had for the new-look Arboretum. A project like the one we had in mind was never going to be free of risk. Risk often brings hesitation, but I didn't hesitate in the least. I always believe everything will work out, and if it doesn't I deal with it. Having weighed up all the pros and cons, I was sure what I was doing was the way forward. Frank, although he is normally more guarded in such matters, didn't resist my line of thinking. I sometimes joke with him that if I decided to flip Arboretum around 180 degrees just for the sake of it, he'd agree with me.

By 2005 our expansion plans had come to fruition. Customers now entered the premises through a new glass atrium into a world of plants, just like today. I used the first five to ten metres of the entrance space for what

I hoped would be enticing tasters of what could be created in a garden. As a passionate plantswoman, I had always imagined visitors entering our shop through a profusion of spectacular plants so they would have no doubt that they were in a garden centre. They would then exit through a profusion of houseplants so that their last memories of Arboretum would once again be plants, together with a warm goodbye and an invitation to call again.

Due to the somewhat unexpected success of our restaurant, the new-look Mulberry's was much bigger, with four times the seating capacity, and some of this seating in a beautiful light-filled, partly covered conservatory. In addition to the restaurant, we built a new, larger conference room. The original had proved to be a success; it had been used by businesses and organisations, including banks and local authorities, from the area and further afield.

This was not the only innovation we introduced during these works. We began experimenting with ancillary offerings in the form of franchise agreements. We built large premises at the entrance to the site and took in a number of businesses that were complementary to our offering. One was lawnmower and tool sales and another was hot tub sales. In this way we were able to offer these complementary product lines even though we did not have the manpower or the knowledge to provide them ourselves. It transpired that some of the franchisees fell victim to the economic crash of 2008 but, for a number of years, they added to our offering and attracted the type of customer who was a natural fit for what we had in our store.

While I had put my heart and soul into these projects, there was one I had misgivings about. Arboretum had at the time a pet shop with live animals and pet products. Such things were very popular before the financial crash of 2008 and the enterprise was successful. I had never been fully happy with the idea of stocking live animals – animals that had to be kept in cages – but had sanctioned it because fish tanks were all the rage at the time. We had employed a manager to run the operation and he was stocking all sorts of creatures that gave me the creeps. We had fish, rats, gerbils and even snakes. Once I looked into a cage and saw what I thought was a statue of an iguana only for it to open its eyes and give me a hard stare. I nearly had a heart attack. When I saw the reality of animals being locked up, I became even more uncomfortable. I reached breaking point when I found out that a snake had escaped and was found in the roof. That was when we decided to keep only cat food, dog food, cat beds and dog kennels, and the other products needed to keep healthy animals. I am convinced that if my heart is not in a project, it is more difficult to make it work.

If stocking live animals does not sit well with me, neither does the celebration of Halloween, because tombstones, blood, gore and monsters are not what Arboretum is about. So, instead of celebrating Halloween in the usual way, we started a tradition in which a storyteller entertains children with fabulous tales with an anti-bullying message. One of the most popular is called Spookley the Square Pumpkin. Hot chocolate is provided for the children, who sit on bales of straw, and parents love both the setting and the message.

By the time of our expansion in 2005, Fergal had taken to the company like a duck to water. His crash was now just a memory but the stress and worry it had caused me were to feature once more. Frank had had a horrible growth on his back for some time and I was always urging him to go to a doctor. Eventually he gave in, and his doctor sent him to a specialist in Kilkenny. However, on the day he was supposed to go to the specialist, he went to the races in Gowran instead. He was found out, of course, because his doctor rang me to say he had missed his appointment. I insisted that he make another with the specialist, and when he drove off to attend I followed him in my car just to make sure he did. The specialist diagnosed a very rare and aggressive form of cancer and Frank was sent straight to hospital.

When the tumour was removed we had to wait for two weeks for the results of the biopsy. These were the two longest weeks of my life. The fear was that the cancer had reached the bone marrow, but it hadn't, thank God. Next was the chemotherapy. Frank was extremely ill on chemotherapy, lost his hair and could not control the tear ducts in his eyes. He became almost unrecognisable, to the point that my niece's husband, who knew him, once had to ask who he was. Later Professor John McCaffrey, Frank's wonderful oncologist, told me he had given Frank the heaviest dose of chemotherapy he had ever given to anybody because Frank was very fit and could take it.

Frank's illness was the most difficult time of my life. When he was too sick to leave the house, he used to ask why I was not in the garden centre making sure everything was running smoothly, but I wanted to be in the house with him. When I would cross the yard into the centre, I would grit my teeth and say to myself, 'Put on the mask and pretend everything is OK.'

Aside from my anguish over what Frank was going through, I was worried about the many families depending on a wage packet from Arboretum. I couldn't let them down. It was also difficult for me that everyone felt they had to ask how Frank was. In one such case, a woman whom I'm sure didn't mean to hurt me inquired about his health and then proceeded to tell me that three of her family members had had cancer, thoughtlessly adding that none of them had survived. I walked away into the safety of the storeroom and cried my eyes out.

Frank was an excellent patient with a positive outlook on his illness. 'We're here for a good time, not for a long time,' he would often joke. He made it easier for us to carry on, personally and in business. We had great support from our families and from our wonderful friends, including Michael and Anne Buggie, Jim Bolger, George Mullins, Eddie Kearney, Willie Mullins, Michael Hosey and Bobby Quinn. We also received tremendous support from our families and Frank's doctor, Tom Foley. Noeleen Doyle, our housekeeper, was especially helpful. When I was struggling to keep the wheels turning, she would make a cup of tea, sit me down and say, 'Ray, how are you doing?' I really appreciated this kindness. It is typical of Noeleen. I relied heavily on my faith at the time and trusted that God would spare Frank and that, despite his bleak prognosis, he would not be taken from us.

While Frank was ill, Barry was attending Horticulture College at the National Botanic Gardens in

Glasnevin in Dublin. He was frequently excused from his studies so that he could visit his Dad who was in a nearby hospital and I know that helped both of them. During Barry's time at Glasnevin, on one of his placements, Barry worked with a landscape company in Dublin. He liked this aspect of Horticulture and when he qualified he set up a landscaping business in the Arboretum. He built up a good business that is still successful today and is run by a colleague from his college days and a neighbour, William Ryan. William came to work with us in 1998 as a very young man. He eventually went away to study Horticulture and returned to us when he qualified. He is like a family member and I frequently refer to him as my adopted third son. Barry, who has worked in every aspect of our enterprise, has developed into a fine businessman and a good people person. He is now Chief Executive Officer of the Arboretum.

Rachel's Reflection

To every problem, there is a solution. However, we have to want that solution and have the courage to take a leap of faith to follow our vision.

Beanstalk', which started my creative juices flowing. I visualised a pond at the bottom of the area designated for the garden, close to the river, and it was to represent the large seed of the beanstalk. Paths resembling huge stalks would radiate from the pond up the slope.

I had many hopes for this garden. Uniting all of these was the idea that Arboretum would be a destination store. By 'destination store', I mean a place to which people are willing to make a special trip, solely for the purpose of shopping there. This is something I had learned from garden centres in the UK. To be a destination store, we needed to offer something unique. I believed that if we created beautiful gardens in which customers could stroll in contemplation, either alone or with friends and family, we would give them an additional reason to hop into the car and make a special trip. It would be an extra motivation on top of our high-quality stock, restaurant and ethos of really looking after our customers. These gardens would serve another important purpose: they would allow customers to see what the plants in our centre looked like in mature form, enabling them to visualise how they might eventually look in their own gardens. The businesswoman in me hoped that, by showing our visitors how mature plants and garden features such as ponds, statues, paths and levels could work together, I could inspire them to purchase pond items, statues and so on in addition to plants. With the basic concept nailed down, I had enormous fun designing the other elements.

A description of the Inspirational Gardens will not do them justice, so I invite you to come and see them. However, I want to mention just a few features that mean a lot to me. When I was studying horticulture in Termonfeckin, the effect of plant colour on mood was not mentioned but it was something I became interested in subsequently. I was determined to share the philosophy. The planting in the Inspirational Gardens favours colours that have a positive effect on people's wellbeing. I placed a large sign at the entrance describing how the different colours stimulate different qualities:

> *Red is for vitality, love and fertility – a great energiser. It helps us to cope with the demands of life. It removes negativity and promotes courage.*
>
> *Green is for growth and harmony. The colour of nature, it is neither warming nor cooling. It brings about change and encourages hope. It's restful and relaxing.*
>
> *Orange is for optimism and joy. It promotes a feeling of wellbeing. A warm and welcoming colour, it inspires optimism and sociability. It provokes change, creates opportunity, enthusiasm and freedom.*

Yellow is for contentment. It represents the power of the sun. It is useful for the shy and the lonely in that it invokes feelings of optimism and self-worth and lifts depression.

Blue is for spirit. It encourages relaxation and tranquillity. It lends itself to meditation and contemplation and evokes patience and calm. It has a cooling and cleansing effect on mind and body.

Purple is for knowledge. It encourages the feeling of self-worth. It is the colour that helps one gain insight into oneself.

My hope was that the garden would inspire our customers to incorporate colour in their own garden designs for its impact on their wellbeing.

In one part of the gardens, I placed several standing stones from the local quarry in Old Leighlin. This is an acknowledgement of our history and a nod to my home county, where ancient standing stones dot the landscape. There is an especially famous dolmen, the Brownshill dolmen, in Carlow. It is the largest portal tomb in Europe and has a capstone weighing around 150 tonnes.

The Inspirational Gardens are punctuated by alluring sculptures: a stone head that looks as if it came all the way from Easter Island, a herd of impala deer far away from their native Africa, and a flock of herons, which might be more local. And the area is full of trees: silver birch (*Betula pendula*), holly (*Ilex*), eucryphia, parrotia, ginkgo, liquidambar, liriodendron, laburnum, crab apple and robinia. There are eleven different types of mountain ash (*Sorbus*) and many beeches (*Fagus*), from spreading to fern-leaf and fastigiate. Magnificent

Magnolia grandiflora treats us to a show of glorious white flowers.

The pond is full of fish and is carefully guarded by stout railings. The fish are koi, a species of beautifully coloured and patterned carp. Ours are Kōhaku, which have a white body and red markings. In Japan they are a symbol of love and friendship. People are amazed when I tell them that I brought these koi with me when we moved from Carlow in 2000, which puts them at a respectable age already, but koi are known for their extraordinarily long lifespan. In the wild they live around fifteen years. However, where they are protected from predators and cared for, as in our pond, they can survive up to forty years. Scientists have examined one particularly long-lived Japanese koi, called Hanako, concluding she lived for 226 years! They are an intelligent species and it is said that they learn to recognise their carers. It makes me smile to think they might recognise me as I show people around, or, more likely, Ger Heary, one of our wonderful horticulturists, who feeds them!

In the middle of the pond I installed a sculpture of four children. It cost £8,000 years ago but I loved it so much I had to have it. Unfortunately, the smallest of the children is missing, presumed drowned. There is a lifebuoy at the pond in case someone topples in, and I'm afraid to say that some bold but inventive individual used it as a lasso and dragged down the little one.

There are more strange creatures in the garden, though these are not living. A crocodile rests among the bamboos while a hippopotamus lolls in the border near the pond. These are sculptures that I picked up on my travels. Many were made in Africa from old cars. A strange pelican-like bird is resting among the phormiums, while up on the hill, in the African section, a huge gorilla watches over the whole scene.

We have a Japanese section in which we've planted Japanese acers and built a Japanese pagoda. Across the path is a white and cream collection of plants, ranging from arum lily *(Zantedeschia)* and hosta 'Krossa Cream Edge' to *Hydrangea paniculata*. In the white and cream collection we grow a very special tree, the Persian ironwood (*Parrotia persica*), whose leaves colour gloriously in autumn.

Children love a maze so I designed a yew maze as the 'top' of the beanstalk, with three large standing stones in the central area. The maze is a win–win for everyone: for kids, who have huge fun in it, and for parents, who can allow their children to run free in it knowing they are safe. It's also a win for Arboretum because the same children are distracted and don't get into mischief in the garden centre, where little fingers sometimes do mischief. Our newly refurbished playground is another big hit. With its little houses, Garda station, kitchen, wigwam, castle, school bus and climbing wall, children love it.

The Inspiration Gardens are high maintenance but this is not always appreciated. I am amused by those people, albeit few, who find pleasure in seeking me out to tell me they have found some weeds in the different beds. I smile and thank them. These small annoyances are worth it when I hear of people who continue to derive great solace from strolling through the gardens. People often tell me about very sick people they know who come to the gardens to walk and sit when they can't do much else. That brings me untold happiness.

Rachel's Reflection

The old saying 'One is nearer to God in a garden than anywhere else on earth' appeals to me.

No Standing Still

The Honey Locust

(*Gleditsia triacanthos*)

This tree is also known as the thorny locust tree. It has graceful leaves and long seed pods. It is highly adaptable to different environments, tolerates poor soil and provides shade.

The financial crash in the autumn of 2008 was ferocious and the rate of unemployment rose to its highest in a decade. No one needs reminding that this brought many to their knees. We, however, were lucky in that we managed to weather the storm and didn't have to let any of our thirty-five or so staff go. Moreover, I was fortunate that Frank had by now made a full recovery. Good fortune, however, could not be depended upon in the midst of what was a deepening recession, and disaster struck just when I thought I had landed on my feet. A golden rule of retail is that your customers should be able to find you, but something happened in 2010 that took us right off the map.

That something was the opening of a new motorway, the M9, taking traffic from the M7 at Kilcullen straight to Waterford and vice versa. On 9 September 2010, when the M9 opened, the road on which our business was located, the N9, became a regional road. This meant that traffic travelling to or from Dublin, Waterford or Kilkenny stopped passing our door. Indeed, none of our non-local customers could find us, resulting in a concerning drop-off in trade. We had our team work very hard on marketing, but, although this helped somewhat, signage remained an issue. The body that controlled national roads projects at the time, the National Roads Authority (now Transport Infrastructure Ireland), adamantly refused to allow us to put up any signage for our premises on the motorway. The pitiful reason it gave was that it would be a distraction for motorists. This was the start of a distressing relationship between our company and the roads authorities that exists to this day.

In addition, there was another, perhaps uniquely Irish, problem – pronunciation. Leighlinbridge is pronounced 'Loughlinbridge', meaning many people were inconvenienced even further in trying to find us.

I remember the moment when I looked at the sales figures and realised the business we had put so much work into building was on the point of collapse. We had to take action or downsize and let staff go – something that was alien to my way of thinking. That morning I had walked into Mulberry's and found it eerily quiet when it should have been loud with customers enjoying breakfast. Enough was enough. I went straight upstairs and marched into the office. 'We really need to talk,' I said to Frank and my sons – Fergal and Barry were by now heavily involved in the business. I'm sure my voice sounded strangled. I was worried, and they all shared my concern. We sat down together in the restaurant and I opened the conversation with a suggestion that we spend a considerable amount of money on signage and branding in an effort to boost the footfall again. The others pointed out that this, even if it worked, wouldn't solve the bottleneck problems we had been having in the restaurant at busy times prior to the motorway opening. As the discussion went on, it became clear that much more than new signs would be needed if we were to become profitable again. We would have to overhaul the restaurant. It just wasn't impressive enough to overcome the new obstacles the M9 had thrown up. There and then, we phoned Barry McCabe, an interior designer specialising in retail, whom we felt was the right person to help us create something 'wow'. We knew Barry McCabe through Retail Excellence Ireland, REI, whose then CEO, David Fitzsimons, was really good to us over the years and was excellent at his job. REI is a representative body for retailers whose aim is to develop top-class retail standards and skills and promote a world-class retail industry in Ireland. World class we wanted to be.

So, from my opening gambit of suggesting we spend €30,000 on branding and signage, we were suddenly talking about considerable works and a considerable spend. Barry McCabe's proposal to give us something 'wow' came in at €750,000. We would require another bank loan. Frank was worried about this but we had a good track record in repaying loans. Furthermore, some rental properties we had purchased during the boom were performing well and could be put up as collateral. Having said that, it was 2010, just two years after the property bubble had burst, and the economy was in freefall. Most accountants would have questioned our judgement on the basis of return on investment but I was looking at the bigger picture. Because I was on the board of Bord Bia – the Irish food development board – I knew exactly what was happening with food culture in Ireland and had a strong sense that serving really high-quality food made with the very best ingredients, preferably local, in a pleasant ambience, was the way we needed to be going.

The new restaurant was to be located at the back of the establishment, not the front. It would seat 340 people and another 100 on the sunny terrace right beside the children's playground and overlooking the Inspirational Gardens and yew maze. It was to be named Rachel's Garden Café. Lest I be accused of having grandiose ideas about my importance to either the family or the enterprise, the name was chosen by my sons in my absence. This was lovely – a tribute to and acknowledgement of my dedication and commitment to the business. I didn't object.

Having grown up on nutritious organic food from my Dad's garden, expertly cooked by my mother, I regard the provenance of food to be of the utmost importance. For this reason, the mission statement for Rachel's

Garden Café reads, 'All our recipes are created with one driving ambition – passion. Whatever we cook, it's because it's the right season, because it's local and because we want to eat it ourselves.'

I was determined to hire the right people for the new restaurant – people who would share its ethos. I had made many mistakes in hiring up to that point in my career. I had sometimes ignored my gut feeling and taken on staff who didn't share my vision or who wouldn't go the extra mile. These were not necessarily bad people but they were just not right for us. While I firmly believe you should hire for attitude, because you can teach skills, I really wanted exceptional chefs for Rachel's Garden Café. Therefore, I asked the candidates to cook a meal as part of their final interviews. Each dish had to be costed, and its shelf life and adaptability noted. We conducted blind testing on everything from coffee to sausages. I love food and consider myself to be a reasonably good cook, so quality and taste were paramount. With this approach to hiring, I was absolutely reassured that our customers would be eating the best of Irish food.

We included in the plans a meeting room, The Herb Garden, which adjoined the new restaurant. It has turned out to be an important adjunct to our business, just as the previous conference rooms had been.

Mothers are used to sons demanding many things of them, but it must have been a first when mine came up to me pleading that I buy them designer urinals for the toilets beside Rachel's Garden Café. Fergal and Barry had accompanied me on a trip to a conference in the UK where we had seen magnificent hand basins and urinals made in the shapes of flowers. They were very taken with the idea. While I have always believed you can judge the calibre of an establishment by the quality of its toilets, I was reluctant to fork out the huge amount of money required to have flower-shaped urinals and hand basins. In the end I caved in, and artist Clarke

Sorenson from San Francisco was commissioned to produce the designs. The purchase proved to be a good decision, not least because the sanitary ware attracted a lot of publicity. A customer who was shepherding US visitors into our establishment was overheard saying she was going to show them Carlow's latest tourist attraction – the toilets at the new Arboretum.

The bright new Rachel's Garden Café was opened by Aidan Cotter, the then chief executive of Bord Bia, on 1 March 2012, within the deadline and two months after the construction work had begun. I waited anxiously for our customers to return. And they did, in droves.

The restaurant overhaul proved to be a very good investment – our footfall counters recorded that 92 percent of customers who entered the establishment went to the restaurant. I hoped that every one of them would be tempted to purchase plants or even furniture on the way out. The café has gone on to win many awards, including the Best Casual Dining in Carlow award from The Restaurant Association of Ireland in 2015 and again in 2020.

Just as the redecoration of one room in a home very often shows up the faults in others, I realised that the upgrade to the restaurant necessitated a look at the rest of the enterprise. Barry, Fergal and I sat down with a plan of the shop and methodically looked at every area. My sons did an analysis of every category and the performance of every product within these categories. Everything from the colour of the paint to the shape of the fixtures and fittings was thoroughly discussed. Out of this analysis a plan emerged that would radically change – and improve – the entire store. Being a garden centre at heart, we started with the plant area.

As I mentioned before, our plants were displayed in the atrium, which is the first part of the building the customer enters, and in an outdoor area directly behind it. Despite the huge variety of plants in the outdoor area, 80 percent of our plant sales happened indoors in the atrium. We deduced this was down to customers not wanting to go outside to look at plants in inclement weather. There was no question of cramming our huge variety of plants and trees into the atrium so we decided we would cover the outdoor plant area, some 2,790 square metres (30,000 square feet). We installed a roof that could be opened or closed depending on the weather. This has proved to be a huge success. The roof can be opened in 70 seconds – quicker than the roofs at Wimbledon tennis club! It makes an interesting sound when opening and closing and adds theatre to the shopping experience.

I should say at this point that I have always visited other garden centres both at home and abroad. Such visits give me the opportunity to see innovative practices in other settings. For example, I saw retractable roofs in operation in Barton Grange and Bents garden centres in the UK. Visits to other garden centres invariably fed my creativity and often provided substance to ideas for Arboretum that were constantly germinating in my fertile mind.

In the course of this major revamp, we talked to our good friends Guy and Carol Topping of Barton Grange, a model garden centre in Preston in the UK. They were always very open to sharing experiences, and when we told them what we were planning they invited us to Preston to see their setup. We accepted their invitation and, as a result of the visit, tweaked our plans to improve customer flow and avoided making an expensive mistake.

We owe our kitchen store, which we developed as part of this revamp, to trips such as the one to Preston. Our UK contemporaries had already observed that kitchen accessories are complementary to our type of business. We borrowed many excellent ideas from Barton Grange and Bents in Warrington.

It didn't all go one way, of course, and we gave advice as readily as we received it, even going so far as to 'lend' our wonderful outdoor manager, Eamonn Wall, to Barton Grange for a week. I remember clearly how it came about. Guy and Carol were in Arboretum on one of the many fact-finding and exchange visits we had. I was showing them around our brand-new plant area and I could see they were impressed. The plants looked very enticing. They were laid out in blocks of colour, as was our plant manager Eamonn Wall's wont. The signage for the plants was just as eye-catching. Again, this was down to our wonderful plant manager and his team. He had written the signs as if the plants were talking to the customers. For example, in the perennials section, where someone might not have known what a herbaceous perennial was, he had put a sign that read: 'We promise to come back every year.' I have always regarded signs and labels as silent salespeople. Most customers like to browse and many dislike being pounced upon by a salesperson, so I believe in providing the answers to their questions before they even have a question. Garden centre personnel from all over the world who come to visit us say our signs are among our many attractions. They provoke conversation and photographs, which, in this age of social media, are very valuable. Our toilets for the disabled sign reads 'For the less abled'. This too attracts positive commentary.

After a light-hearted discussion on signage, I shared with the Toppings our weekly plant sales figures. Guy stopped in his tracks.

'What did you say the population within a thirty-mile radius of Leighlinbridge is?' he asked.

He was surprised by how many plants we sold given that we were located in a fairly rural area far from a major city. Barton Grange is in Preston, close to Manchester, which has a population on its doorstep of two and a half million, around half of Ireland's. When Guy had recovered sufficiently, he had another question.

'Is there any chance you could lend me your plant sales guy for a week?'

'Of course,' I said, when I had thought it through. 'And in exchange, could we have your head of visual merchandising?'

I had long been envious of the eye-catching and very creative displays I had seen in Barton Grange. Guy agreed to my request, so preparations began to send Eamonn Wall to Preston and bring Barton Grange's display manager, David Fawcett-Ropner, to Leighlinbridge.

Eamonn arrived at Barton Grange on a bitterly cold St Patrick's weekend with an open mind and a willingness to impart his expertise and learn from the Barton Grange team. His first observation was that when the gates opened, the customers flooded in – so different from Arboretum, where we constantly need to remind our customers that we exist. However, Eamonn was on exchange for a reason and he got to work.

Through his observations and recommendations, sales in the plant area at Barton Grange increased by 5 percent during his time there.

We loved having David Ropner-Fawcett here with us in Leighlinbridge and admired his get-up-and-go. If he felt a coffee or lunch break was going on too long, he would clap his hands and say, 'Let's crack on.' And crack on we did. I had picked out the members of our team I felt had the most promise when it came to visual merchandising and assigned them to David. There were a number of girls who showed real potential in this area and were well able to absorb the information David shared as he worked. As the week went on, we could see there were a few stars who showed flair for merchandising. Though I had already felt we should be doing more with visual merchandising – that was why I had asked for David – it was really his visit and seeing the potential and enthusiasm that crystallised my thoughts. Soon after, Nicole Foley joined our team and we supported her in developing her skills in visual merchandising. It didn't stop there: Nicole is now purchasing manager and is still our head visual merchandiser. At Christmastime, in particular, she is worth her weight in gold. I love developing our team members and promoting from within.

The Barton Grange exchange, and indeed the open relationship we have with many garden centres, goes to show how beneficial networking can be in business. Around this time, another very tangible benefit emerged: our English garden centre friends suggested that we join their buying group in order to 'piggyback' on their buying power. This has been excellent for us as it has given us a competitive edge because of the volume of sales going through their group. I strongly believe that networking is the single most important piece in the jigsaw of business.

We employed an excellent electrician, Damien Byrne, during this revamp, who worked on a lighting plan determining what type of lighting was suitable for every product. The result was a revelation to us. Not only did we get an excellent lighting system in our business but we also managed to reduce our electrical consumption costs by a considerable amount.

We added another new department in the course of the 2010 revamp, but, before I get into it, I need to give you some background. In 2008 we had invited Edinburgh Woollen Mill to trade on our site. You will recall we had downgraded our pet shop. This meant we were able to offer Edinburgh Woollen Mill the area the pet shop had occupied plus the old conference room. Edinburgh Woollen Mill stocks popular brands of women's, men's and children's clothing at competitive prices. We were interested in it because it caters for an older female customer – one of our sweet-spot customer personas because she is also interested in gardening and is a good customer for the café. This has been a really positive relationship, going beyond the business. The owner, Philip Day, and his wife, Debbie, have become friends of our family, as has the manager and chief executive officer, Steve Simpson, and his wife, Julie. They are regular visitors to Carlow.

Seeing the success of fashion in the product mix, it wasn't long before we identified an unfulfilled niche in the market: younger women. This is the additional department we decided to add in the 2010 revamp. We had been stocking a range of beautiful oak furniture and felt that we had come to the end of that particular range; we had sold it to anyone who was interested in it. The space it had occupied would be our fashion store. We decided we would stock brands and labels that were exclusive to our area. With that in mind, Barry and I, a pair of horticulturists, more used to manure than couture, headed off to Pure London, a big fashion buying event. In actual fact, buying fashion is not dissimilar to buying plants. There was an important difference, though: whereas we wanted most of our plants to be familiar to our customers, we were on the lookout for fashion brands that were unknown. We sourced exciting names in apparel and accessories such as jewellery, handbags and scarves. We guessed quantities, using our gut instinct. As this was our first time buying fashion, that was all we could do.

I remember going to Coventry after Pure London to give a talk for the Garden Centre Association, the UK's industry association, on 'busting queues in restaurants'. I felt like a fraud – I was neither a restaurateur nor a fashion buyer! After the talk, which went very well, I went straight to Glee, the UK's biggest garden and outdoor living trade show, and I was back in my comfort zone again.

I am glad to say that ladies' fashion performed well for us from the start. We were soon approached by Regatta, the outdoor clothing brand, to stock its range. We recognised that this was catering for another type of customer, namely those who like to partake in outdoor activities like hiking. For a number of years it added to our appeal as a destination.

If you'd told me that morning in 2010 when I walked into an empty Mulberry's that within the year we'd have refocused, reinvested, redesigned, redeveloped, re-energised, re-engaged and relaunched, I'd have laughed; but that's exactly what we did. Our response to the crisis cost over €2 million. We also ended up spending that €30,000 on marketing and branding to tell people about our wonderful café, the Herb Garden meeting room, the extended plant area, the new-look store and new departments. The investment was risky in the middle of a countrywide financial depression, but I saw it differently. In business you either go backwards or forwards. There is no standing still.

Rachel's Reflection

We have always been problem solvers, growing, developing and empowered, in spite of challenges. We have never been cowed or overcome by challenges.

Work and Play with the IGCA

The Blackthorn (*Prunus spinosa*)
This tree had much symbolism and mythology associated with it. It was regarded as an omen of bad luck and the consequences of it being cut down were feared.

I'll never forget going to my first meeting of the board of the International Garden Centre Association (IGCA). I was about to give a country report for Ireland and the sweat was rolling down my back. It wasn't the Kentucky heat that was making me sweat; it was fear. I was a woman in what was then a man's world, with a country flag in front of me as if I were at a meeting of the United Nations General Assembly.

The chairman of the association – Lord rest him – was a flamboyant Dutchman who knew how to command attention, and when he first spotted me at the meeting he bounded up to me and shook my hand, saying, 'You have to be Rachel from Ireland.' Of course I was Rachel from Ireland; I was the only woman in the room. The chairman was so considerate and, probably because he saw I was scared out of my life, facilitated me by proposing to hear all country reports anticlockwise. Since there were only two other delegates ahead of me, this meant I was able to relax and enjoy the rest of the experience when I had given my report.

Despite the fact that horticulture was male dominated, and despite the little instances of sexism I had experienced early in my career, I have to say that male colleagues, including those in the IGCA, typically treated me with the utmost respect. Little did I know when I first heard of the IGCA, through the late Michael Devitt of Newlands Garden Centre, that it would enrich my life and career so much.

The association, as its name suggests, is an international organisation for owners of garden centres, and its purpose is to provide a global forum for the mutual exchange of information and ideas. Its membership consists of twenty-two national garden centre associations from around the world. It is committed to seeing the overall improvement of the garden centre industry, which it achieves by organising garden centre visits, workshops, lectures, exchange programmes and social events. It also organises annual congresses.

Congress is held in a different member country each year and involves a weeklong programme of talks, garden centre visits, sightseeing and cultural events, in addition to offering a golden opportunity to network. I attended my first Congress in Toronto in Canada in 1995. It was an unforgettable trip, so much so that I have never missed a Congress since. It inspired me to become a board member of the association the following year, when I was invited to do so. Being a member has brought Arboretum innumerable benefits, and many of the innovations I made in my business resulted from my seeing them in operation in other countries. It is such an honour that my son Fergal is now a board member of the international association. Barry's first experience of Congress was in the year he did his leaving certificate exams, when the event was held in the Netherlands. He has been a regular since.

In 2008, when on my way to Japan for the association's winter board meeting, I was aware that there was a slot for Congress to be held in a European country in 2014, considering that the 2013 Congress had been allocated to Australia. At the time, I was a member of the horticultural board in Bord Bia, the State board for the promotion of food and horticulture, and I approached the then CEO of the agency, Aidan Cotter, with a proposal.

'Would Bord Bia support the industry if I succeeded with a bid to host Congress in Ireland in 2014?' I asked, unsure of how Aidan would react given Ireland's bleak economic prospects at the time.

'Yes, Rachel,' he said. 'We should be well out of recession by then.'

I admired his optimism. I suppose that, for him, Congress was going to tick many boxes in that it would showcase Ireland as a food island and promote not only its horticulture but also its vibrant history and culture. So, with the blessing of Bord Bia, I put forward a bid and was successful. It would mean embarking on three years of preparations for the event from 2011 onwards.

I guess I must have made my mark at meetings of the IGCA because in 2013 I was greatly honoured to be elected as its president for the period 2014 to 2015. I was inaugurated at the Congress in Melbourne, Australia, and was very pleased when another Carlow native, Noel White, the then Irish ambassador to

Australia, flew in from Canberra for the occasion. I was thrilled that my family could also be there, along with Mike Neary and Carol Marks of Bord Bia.

Since my early days in the business I have always been conscious of the importance of networking. In 2014, when I had become president of the IGCA, I set out that one of my ambitions during my two-year term would be to increase the number of countries in the membership of the association. To that end I asked delegates to recommend a contact in China. A Japanese colleague, Koachi Akatsuta, gave me the name of one such person – Larry Lee. We invited Larry to come from China to Ireland when it was our turn to host the international Congress in 2014. He accepted and has been in Ireland many times since. Indeed, Barry and I have been to visit him in China several times. We have made a valuable business contact and we now purchase some of our garden furniture directly from China, bypassing the United Kingdom, cutting out the middleman and simplifying the currency exchanges. We now have exclusive products and can maintain our margins while giving our customers better value for money. This has meant that Brexit has not been as catastrophic as it could have been from a supply-chain point of view, although, believe me, it has thrown up many other challenges.

Relationships in business are built up through networking, and the trust and loyalty that result from this are important. When we visit China, Barry and I always request to see the factories to ensure the furniture is produced ethically. On our first visit we were amazed to see how the weave material was made and surprised that all the tables and chairs were handmade. I had always assumed that, in this era, such work would be done by machines. I now have a greater appreciation of the craft and the workmanship that has gone into making every single piece of that style of garden furniture we sell.

There are many wonderful people in the IGCA who helped me during my presidency, but one in particular was the administrator, a Canadian called Victor Santacruz. He promptly answered all my emails and phone calls and made my presidency easy. His commitment to our industry and to horticulture across Canada is outstanding. He and his wife, Lauren, are friends for life.

Hosting Congress in Ireland in 2014 was one of the highlights of my presidency, and of my career. The work involved in organising it consumed me for several years but I was so lucky that my two sons were able to assist on the steering committee. Having by then become directors in Arboretum, they were able to keep the business running smoothly and allow me to be more hands-off. The steering committee comprised Fergal, Barry and me, as well as Mike Neary and Carol Marks from Bord Bia. Also on board was Eoin Reid, owner of

Fernhill Garden Centre in Athlone. Frank was a rock in supporting us in every way.

The Irish Congress, which was held in Carton House, Maynooth, County Kildare, has gone down in the annals of the IGCA as one of the most successful ever. The President of Ireland, Michael D. Higgins, was kind enough to take time out of his busy schedule to speak to the delegates at a black-tie event in Dublin's Mansion House. The 250 delegates, from twenty-two countries, were most impressed by his speech and his respect for those who, as he put it, 'knew how to put their hands into the soil of Ireland'.

The Congress itinerary included a superb guided tour of the historic Glasnevin Cemetery, whose history had been unknown to me prior to a pre-Congress visit. We had superb guides on the day. The Guinness Storehouse was next on the list and proved to be very popular. We also visited Croke Park, home of the Gaelic Athletic Association; the National Botanic Gardens, Glasnevin;

the Jameson Distillery, Bow St.; and the Japanese Gardens and St Fiachra's Garden, both at the Irish National Stud in Kildare. Malahide Castle and Gardens and Kilkenny Castle Park and Gardens were also on our visiting list.

I was determined not to let the delegates go home without visiting several Irish garden centres including, of course, Arboretum in Leighlinbridge. Following the visit we had lunch at the Lyrath Estate, Kilkenny, where we had arranged for industry producers interested in exportation, including nurseries, bulb growers and Christmas tree growers, to meet potential customers. This was an extremely worthwhile event, and numerous business contacts were made at it.

After the visit to Kilkenny Castle gardens and a trip on the Kilkenny Road Train, we headed to a race meeting in Gowran Park, in County Kilkenny. It was a beautiful evening, the sun was shining, and the racecourse looked splendid. Frank acted as the 'tipster' on the day. No better man. It was a Congress of firsts: it was the first time the delegates had visited a race meeting, the first time they had visited a cemetery, and, indeed, the first time they were addressed by a country's head of state.

Following the races, we hosted the closing event of the day in Arboretum, where, after the close of business, the Arboretum team had transformed the plant area into a stage for a production of Riverdance and the restaurant into a banquet hall.

The Carlow choir Aspiro, under the baton of Mary Amond O'Brien, provided dinnertime entertainment. The choir members were dressed in the uniform of Rachel's Garden Café and started to sing flash-mob style while dinner was being served. I will never forget that moment. They gave a gorgeous rendition of the wonderful old Irish song 'Danny Boy' and everyone fell silent to listen. Then Kyle, the son of our good friend Kieran Dunne, a fellow nurseryman, gave an impressive rendition of three more beautiful songs. Our challenge then was to move our guests to the next entertainment – the performance of Riverdance that was to be staged in the plant area. Given what had come before them, the Riverdance troop had their work cut out for them. They didn't let us down.

It was truly a magical evening, and delegates have shared their memories of it with me at every Congress since. The Congress was considered to have been a huge success and I know we did Ireland proud. It was also a financial success owing to sponsorship from suppliers to the trade and to the work of the committee members who gave so willingly of their time, creativity and energy. Our main sponsor was Westland Horticulture. The profit made was put into an account in Bord Bia and has been used to help market our industry. I asked for €10,000 to be ring-fenced so we would have money to pay Ireland's membership subscription to the IGCA for years to come.

BRANCHES

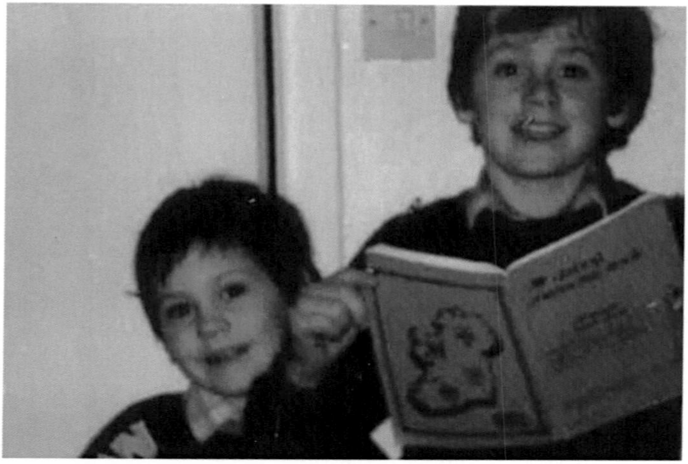

Fergal and Barry at their homework

Arboretum in Carlow

Arboretum and the River Burren that flooded

The roof of our new home when we bought it

House and nursery in Leighlinbridge

House with new roof

The Crusade for Kilquade

The Willow (*Salix alba*)

To the ancient Celts the willow was the tree of enchantment and mystery. It was believed to promote and increase psychic powers, dreams and intuition.

Some things just happen out of the blue. In the spring of 2014, I received an unexpected call from Niall Power, the owner of the National Garden Exhibition Centre, in Kilquade, County Wicklow. It wasn't a personal call; he wanted to talk business.

'Rachel, I'm going to have to sell Kilquade. Would you be interested? I think you'd be a great person to take over the site.'

It sounded like flattery, and I wasn't going to be talked into anything I hadn't even been thinking about. After all, the exhibition centre was no small operation for anyone to take on. It had a restaurant, shop, nursery and twenty permanent gardens to be maintained. These gardens were designed by leading designers between the 1960s and 1990s and each had a unique story to tell. The centre had a reputation among gardeners for the quality and rarity of the plants it grew, sourced and sold.

‘So, what do you think?’

‘Thank you, Niall, but I really have enough problems in my life with one garden centre; I don’t think I could cope with a second,’ I responded.

'Don’t rule it out; think about it,’ Niall concluded, and after a bit of small talk hung up the phone.

Niall rang a few more times in the following months but my reply was always the same. However, the seed was sown, and very soon afterwards the conditions were almost good enough for it to sprout. Towards the end of August, I discovered that Kilquade was advertised in the property sections of the leading newspapers. Fergal, who had been *en route* to a conference in Italy, had contacted me to let me know. I hopped into my car and drove to the nearest petrol station, bought a copy of *The Irish Times* and leafed through it for the property supplement. And there it was, an article on Kilquade. 'The exhibition centre,' it stated, 'is a well-established brand with obvious potential to grow and develop the business even further.' It was speaking my kind of language. I put the newspaper down and telephoned both Frank and Barry.

'Let's go take a look,' I said to each of them.

I needed to get it out of my system, and I think they wanted that too.

When we drove to Wicklow to look at the property, Barry told me to wear sunglasses so nobody would recognise me as I explored the property. I took my sunglasses out of my bag, put them on and walked into the little shop to look at the retail setup. However, no sooner had I walked in the door than I heard the words of a woman I had been to college with: 'Rachel Candy, what are you doing here?' My cover was blown.

After a chat with Susan, a former classmate, I walked around the gardens. It's safe to say I fell in love! I was thrilled to see that the four seasons were portrayed compellingly, with different themes and eras represented. My brain started to whirr with ideas as I strolled along each of the winding paths, and although the gardens were somewhat neglected, I was in awe of their old-world charm and eclectic mix of styles, from Gothic to Feng Shui. I was particularly enchanted by the Harlequin Walk, with its alternating bands of copper and green beech. At the end of the main walk was the Neo-Georgian Wall, which provided a satisfying focal point, that focal point being Irish sculptor Fiona Coffey's double-headed water serpent, from whose blue-fanged mouths water trickled into a pool. Nearby the vibrant pinks and reds of a rose garden were reflected in the central, circular pond. Being a fan of garden art, I fell for the many designer pieces placed perfectly to catch the eye. To me, the gardens, with their gorgeous scents, colours and textures, encapsulated everything good about gardening and nature.

But did the men in my life need more convincing? I watched Frank and Barry as they walked the gardens and I could see that Barry was very impressed, despite what he later described as an air of neglect. Frank, although he could see great potential, was a little slower to come round.

'How on earth are we going to manage two garden centres?' he asked, in his usual down-to-earth way.

'That's not a problem,' I said. 'We managed to get to where we are today, so what's another centre? We'll get good people in and train them in our ethos and we'll be successful.'

A bit of positivity did the trick. When Fergal returned from his trip to Italy, we arranged another visit to Kilquade. Not least because of his family's enthusiasm, he too agreed that we should put in a bid.

The enterprise was sold by way of a best-bid system, meaning all the interested parties had to submit a bid by 5 p.m. on a specific Friday evening. We put in ours at the very last minute, having spent a long time deliberating on the amount. It was a really difficult decision because we were so keen to have the centre but obviously didn't want to offer too much. On the following Monday evening, after the longest weekend of our lives, we learned to our delight that our bid had been accepted.

Deciding to bid was probably the happiest part of the process for me. Subsequently, I found the project to be very challenging. When the sale went through, we promptly got the licence needed to develop the restaurant. Developing it was to be the first undertaking because I knew only too well from Arboretum in Leighlinbridge that food was key to enticing customers through the door. I won't dwell on the nitty-gritty, except to say that having spent €360,000 on the development, our world collapsed.

You might wonder how something could have gone wrong given our experience of upgrading restaurants at Arboretum. Let me explain. In order to disguise our interest in the bidding process, we had employed a solicitor from the greater Dublin area instead of our local one. It turned out that this solicitor hadn't done the due-diligence work on the records of the enterprise and that, unknown to us, Wicklow County Council had issued no less than seven enforcement notices to the previous owner. These notices largely concerned the building of unauthorised structures on the site and the unauthorised use of other buildings – mainly those used by various franchises operating at the centre.

While sorting out the enforcement notices with an alert and alarmed county council, we discovered to our horror that our lovely new, expensive restaurant was the cause of more trouble: the painter who had painted it to brighten it up hadn't used fire-retardant paint, so it had to be repainted with the proper product. Moreover, there were major problems to be sorted out with the sewerage and electricity.

Of the many mountains I had to climb, there was one that I had climbed before, or at least attempted to climb. Very soon after making our purchase in Kilquade, I faced problems with the National Roads Authority's stance on signage, just as I had experienced problems when the new M9 motorway had diverted traffic from the road running past our business in Leighlinbridge. As part of upgrade works on the N11, the National Roads Authority, which in 2015 became known as Transport Infrastructure Ireland, removed a large sign advertising Kilquade that had been *in situ* for over twenty years. This exit sign had greatly assisted customers and its absence continues to cause great confusion. The authority has proved very difficult to deal with.

While I totally understand that the national roads authority cannot sanction a motorway sign for every business, I believe the enterprises in both Kilquade and Leighlinbridge meet its criteria. I still live in hope that common sense will prevail and that it will see the public benefit of reinstating the signage it removed. This is especially the case because the gardens in Kilquade, just like the Inspirational Garden in Leighlinbridge, are tourist attractions that are free of charge to the public. What's more, the Leighlinbridge store has a visitor information point that has been accredited by Fáilte Ireland, the national tourism authority, and is staffed by Arboretum.

We opened the enterprise in Kilquade in 2015, five months later than planned due to all these problems. Had we known it would be so challenging, we might not have bought the place. Having said that, we have been blessed in that it has gone from strength to strength. The restaurant is working well and plant sales are very satisfactory. Since the enterprise has always had a reputation for selling specialist plants, we are working hard to keep them in stock. I try to remember what Ben McCall taught me all those years ago about the importance of looking after customers who depend on you to provide them with products they can't get elsewhere. We're restoring and caring for the gardens on the site, despite ongoing vandalism. For example, I have erected a beautiful sundial known as the Equatorial Dial, designed by renowned designer Gordon Ledbetter. It's a piece of art, and the Kilquade gardens are deserving of it. For me, that will be an ongoing labour of love.

Fergal and Barry are now at the helm, ready for this challenge. I look forward to seeing this magical place developed further as a destination in County Wicklow – the county known as the Garden of Ireland.

I was really proud of the Arboretum Kilquade team when, in November 2022, Retail Excellence Ireland awarded us with the accolade of Garden centre of the Year.

***

On many occasions throughout my life, I have taken opportunities when presented and have had no regrets about any of the resulting ventures. One such opportunity arose just over a year after purchasing Kilquade when an adjoining property, consisting of a house and 7.63 acres of land, came on the market. Since my family and I believed we would never get this opportunity again, we bought it. The house is called 'Hunter's Moon'. It had been the home of a Russian designer, Bayon Ivan Giltsoff, who came to live in Ireland in the 1940s. Giltsoff designed in Kilquade what is now known as the Old Russian Village, an enclave of twenty houses, each with a different design but each having some features in common with the others, such as dark beams, leaded windows and shale roof tiles. Hunter's Moon, which has a garage and stables in addition to its living quarters, would lend itself to many different uses. It has kept me awake at night thinking of all the possibilities it offers.

Rachel's Reflection

Growing a business is not just about surviving but also about adapting, changing, building and evolving – moving over time to places never imagined, on roads without signposts.

High Grades and Accolades

The Oak Family (*Quercus robur*)
Known as the 'King of the Forest', the oak represents all that is noble, strong, true, wholesome and stable. It is also associated with royalty. Ancient British kings wore crowns of oak leaves.

On my desk I have a small plaque given to me by a friend. It carries a quote from the great Italian artist and sculptor Michelangelo: 'I am always learning.' It was given to me because it was thought to be a perfect description of me and something that I often say of myself.

From my earliest years I have yearned to learn more – at my father's knee, at school, when I decided at the age of twenty-two to change career, and when I decided to start a business. I always seek to learn and I'm an unashamed 'course junkie'. During my years at college especially, I developed an unquenchable thirst for all things horticultural, and this desire for knowledge translated into my many and varied interests. Shortly after I married, I enrolled in a nursery-management course in Piltown horticultural college, County Kilkenny. I drove for fifty minutes every Tuesday to get there and enjoyed every second of the course. I have attended evening classes in every subject I could find, from photography to applying make-up. That one amuses me in hindsight as I never have time to apply make-up.

I particularly remember a course that had the not particularly exciting title of 'The Psychology of Achievement' and which was created by the prolific Canadian motivational public speaker and self-development author Brian Tracy. I was impressed by this series of lectures and inspired by the presenter, the late John Butler of the company Century Management. I can remember very well my chagrin when, some time later, when I was myself delivering a talk (on herbs for cooking), my car, containing all the tapes I had carefully collected on the psychology of achievement, was stolen. I'm not sure which was the greater loss, my car or my collection of tapes. I have seen neither of them since.

County and city enterprise boards were established in 1993, a time of high unemployment. They were created to stimulate economic development and foster local entrepreneurship by providing financial and technical supports for the development of small enterprises. I found our local board, Carlow Enterprise Board, to be excellent. The county enterprise boards were dissolved in 2014, and since then similar work has been done by the Local Enterprise Office (LEO). Each county has one. Past and present CEOs – Michael Kelly (County Enterprise Board) and Kieran Comerford (Carlow Local Enterprise Office), respectively – organise and run courses on every aspect of business growth and development and they can always depend on Arboretum to send members of its team to attend. My son Fergal attended a Carlow Enterprise Board management development course delivered by Blaise Brosnan. He was so impressed by the lecturer and the course that I decided I would have to experience it for myself. I enrolled for Blaise's next course and found that what Fergal had reported to me was true. Barry attended the course too and also found it extremely positive. My sons and I had found a genius who is now not only an adviser to and critic of our business but also a personal friend to all of us. He is the perfect gentleman, quiet, respectful of other opinions, analytical in his summaries and expert at reaching consensus where there are conflicting views. I have taken a lot from his three successful books: *You Are the Limiting Factor*, *Jack*, and *I Dare You – Get it Right in Your Own Head First*. I use many of his phrases in my work. 'What gets written gets done' is one of his sayings that I have adopted. Our family values his capabilities and his friendship. The lunches we share can go on for a long time.

When our original Arboretum was in its infancy, I attended one of my first business development courses with Plato, Carlow. Plato was an organisation that promoted the development of small indigenous businesses. There were several Plato groups around the country. The programme was led by managers from large companies in the county, and I was fortunate to have Paddy Byrne from Burnside Engineering as my mentor. Paddy is a perfect gentleman, friend and a very astute businessman. The programme facilitated the sharing of experiences and resources and provided a safe and confidential forum to develop business and management skills. It was both a superb networking platform and a training facility. I regarded Plato as highly practical. Participants decided on the topic for each session and had open discussions about the challenges they faced. In the 1990s many owners and managers found themselves isolated and unsure where to access expertise. Plato filled that void.

In 1998 I decided to take one day a week away from Arboretum. I felt I needed time off to do something totally different from the gardening business. Looking back, I think I was feeling somewhat overloaded and needed the headspace. The escape I chose was a course in social studies, which was offered in St. Patrick's College in Carlow – a third-level college and seminary. I found it interesting and it was an entirely new experience for me. It taught me so much. I found myself reading books about a wide range of social problems, including eye-opening material on women in poverty. Before that, I would never have thought of reading such material. One of the projects I was tasked with required me to work with a community organisation in Carlow. I chose to work with the Traveller people. Working with them made me aware of their culture and way of life and how we, the general public, try to impose our way of life on them. I believe that interaction between the settled community and Traveller people is a two-way street and that there must be mutual respect. We should obey the tenet, 'Do unto others as you would like them to do to unto you.'

Every year, Retail Excellence Ireland – a not-for-profit company that supports Irish retailers to be the best they can be – runs a two-day course described as a retail retreat. Each year all the Arboretum directors attend, and our managers attend on one or both days. It is always a worthwhile event, with inspirational speakers and many opportunities to network. It is a part of our training and networking calendar that we all look forward to. REI is an exceptionally good representative body for the retail industry. We are extremely lucky to have it. I must acknowledge the leadership of all the CEOs of the REI in my time and give a particular mention to the latest, Duncan Graham, who has led us effectively through the challenging circumstances of the coronavirus pandemic. He brings a new perspective and I look forward to seeing where it takes us as an industry.

***

Perhaps inspired by Dad winning his Muintir na Tíre gardening awards in the mid-1970s, I have entered Arboretum in many competitions. The work involved in making submissions to competitions has been worth it as, over the years, the business has received many awards, and I have even received some. In 1991, Bord Glas (which merged with Bord Bia in 2004) decided to create an awards system to help raise the standards in our industry. This was an excellent programme and helped all of us in the industry to improve the quality of our businesses. For the period 2002 to 2003, Arboretum won the Garden Centre of the Year award. We were ecstatic on receiving such an accolade. In 2005 and 2006, the Department of Agriculture in Northern

Ireland and our own Department of Agriculture and Bord Bia joined together to make this an all-Ireland award. We travelled to Belfast for the award ceremony and came home with the top prize – the All-Ireland Garden Centre of the Year award. This encouraged us to be competitive in protecting our position, and for many years thereafter we won the Bord Bia Garden Centre of the Year and Best Customer Service awards. We have also picked up trophies in everything from plant merchandising and human resources to product information and signage. Our team have truly earned these awards through their commitment and dedication and the respect they have for each other and their customers.

While all the personal honours I have received are special to me, one I cannot go without mentioning is the European Personality of the Year award, which I received from Graine d'Or in the Lido in Paris. That this was given to me in recognition of my international work during my presidency of the IGCA means so much to me. Another award deserving of mention is my lifetime achievement award from County Carlow Chamber of Commerce for my contribution to business in the county. There is nothing nicer than getting recognition on your own turf.

Where my proud moments on the podium are concerned, being a finalist in the EY Entrepreneur of the Year programme in 2018 was the icing on the cake. The programme is run by global accountancy firm Ernst & Young. As its name suggests, it encourages entrepreneurship among all those with potential who demonstrate vision, leadership and success and recognises the contribution of those who inspire and encourage others. It is the only global awards programme of its kind and reaches more than 145 cities in over sixty countries.

In Ireland candidates for the award may be nominated by other business people or members of the public. I was fortunate to have been nominated in the industry category by two friends, who had previously been finalists. After being nominated, there follows a rigorous three-part shortlisting process. The first involves an interview with a number of the EY team at which it is decided whether you may proceed to the next stage. In the second part, you have to answer a comprehensive list of questions on all aspects of your business, give a complete disclosure of your company's financial stability and declare that all due taxes have been paid. In the third part, you have to go through a penetrating interview with a panel of twelve judges who have all the details about you and your business. It was daunting but also exciting and invigorating. In the end, a shortlist of twenty-four candidates was chosen from a total of 110, and I was lucky to be among them.

The gala awards were held in Citywest and I was deeply honoured to have been a finalist. More than 1,500 businesspeople from across the country were in attendance to celebrate our achievements. The experience opened up a world of amazing people, and I feel so privileged to have been able to join the network of EOY alumni, the name given to all the finalists from previous years – people considered to be on top of their game.

Each year the alumni attend an annual CEO retreat. In 2018, the year I was a finalist, this was held in both Oxford and London. This was a week of learning from and networking with the best. I heard talks by well-known personalities, and my favourite speakers included the golfer Paul McGinley, who gave an excellent presentation on the principles of leadership, team building and diversity. Lord Karan Bilimoria, the founder of Cobra Beer, impressed me with his story of the many challenges he faced on his way to success. I thoroughly enjoyed a musical event in a beautiful church in Oxford. I had breakfast with the other alumni one morning at the House of Lords and later that day attended a reception in the Irish embassy, followed by dinner in the evening in Kensington Palace. This is a flavour of the kinds of events organised at EOY retreats.

In 2019 our CEO retreat was held in Hong Kong and Shenzhen in mainland China, and that was the trip of a lifetime. Had COVID-19 not intervened, we would have been in Capetown in South Africa in 2020. Our 2021 retreat was held in Killarney, with a superb lineup of speakers. My favourite after-dinner speaker in Killarney was Alastair Campbell, the British broadcaster and journalist perhaps best known for his role as press secretary and communications strategist for Tony Blair when he was leader of the Labour Party.

The combined revenue of the EOY alumni is €23 billion and the total employee headcount is 200,000. It is interesting that 75 percent of us do business with one another. I have learned so much from this business community and feel proud to be part of it.

Rachel's Reflection

Networking is not about just connecting people. It's about connecting people with people, people with ideas, and people with opportunities.

Michele Jennae

As you might expect, I was involved in a variety of organisations connected to my life in horticulture, such as the Garden Centre Association of Ireland, which I chaired, and you already know about my long association with the International Garden Centre Association. I was the chair of the horticultural board in Bord Bia, the Irish Food Board, and I represented horticulture on Bord Bia's main board. Both appointments were made by the Government. I also sat on the audit-and-risk committee of Bord Bia. I have great respect for this organisation, how it functions at all levels and the great work it does to promote the Irish food, drinks and horticultural industries in Ireland and globally. It runs sixteen offices in various countries across the world. I retired from these boards in 2021. However, I still keep in touch with my many friends in Bord Bia and former members of various boards.

But that retirement did not last long. David Walsh asked me to join HaloCare Commercial Advisory

Board and I was delighted to accept. This organisation helps people live a normal life in their own homes and communities through the use of modern technology. I am so pleased to be working with these great people.

My voluntary work and work on committees and boards has reinforced my view that community spirit is alive and well in our small towns and villages. A huge amount of work is done on a voluntary basis. Leighlinbridge has a particularly strong community spirit and that is one of the reasons I love living there. Leighlinbridge has four public gardens, and I am happy to say I was involved in designing all of them. I still don't know if they are a product of community spirit or if community spirit is a product of them. Either way, they are wonderful resources for the village and a testament to the power of working together and thinking big. Everyone whose job is to encourage volunteers or team work can learn from our experience in Leighlinbridge.

The first of Leighlinbridge's four public gardens was its Millennium Garden. It would probably never have happened without the Government's Green Town 2000 awards initiative. With a prize fund of £150,000, the National Millennium Committee hoped the scheme would encourage towns and villages to promote the concept of environmental sustainability at local level.

Our small but vibrant Leighlinbridge Improvement Group thought we should have a pop at it and asked me if I would design a garden to celebrate the millennium year. The committee, chaired by John Meaney, decided a large, triangular plot, situated between two roads and owned by the county council, would be an ideal location. At the time, it was overgrown with poplar trees that were in a dangerous condition and it was an unofficial dumping ground. Although it was an eyesore, I saw its potential.

I began racking my brains for a suitable design, something unique. While driving to a garden awards ceremony where I'd been a judge, I heard a discussion about the peace process in Northern Ireland on my car radio. My career in horticulture more or less coincided with the Troubles. I often heard the news of yet another atrocity as I drove to or from the garden centre or travelled to give a class, meet a client or carry out my voluntary work. I was at last hearing good news from the North on the radio – the Good Friday Agreement had been signed. A seed was sown in my mind: we would create a peace garden in Leighlinbridge. In the following weeks and months, my idea came together. The Millennium Garden would consist of a series of gardens to symbolise our hopes for the new millennium: peace, happiness, friendship, reconciliation, hope, harmony and eternity. These mini-gardens would each feature particular trees and shrubs, and stone in some form from the local quarry at Old Leighlin, a nearby village. For example, in the 'hope' mini-garden a stone obelisk is surrounded by flowering almonds (*Prunus dulcis*), hawthorn (*Crataegus monogyna*) and snowdrops (*Galanthus nivalis*). In the botanical world each of these plants and bulbs is the first to flower in its respective season. Together they represent true hope in our lives.

In addition to the stone feature in each mini-garden, there is a stone plinth with a very short description of that garden engraved on it, naming the plants that characterise it. All the stones were donated by the building firm Sisk, which owned the quarry. Fr Tom Lalor, our parish priest, suggested there was space on the stones for a quotation in addition to the description. We approached the late Charlie McGuinn, a Leighlinbridge resident, who chose relevant quotations for each standing stone. To stay with the 'hope' mini-garden, the quotation is from William Shakespeare's Richard III: '*True hope is swift and flies with swallow's wings*'.

With seven mini gardens to design, this project allowed me to really push my creativity and I put everything into it. I hope you will indulge me in allowing me to share the details of the others.

Garden no. 1: Peace and Tranquillity

Four similar-sized flat stones represent the four provinces of Ireland: Ulster, Munster, Leinster and Connacht. I believe the stone slabs depict the wonders of nature and are representative of peace and tranquillity as we develop in the womb. This garden is partly surrounded by Peace Roses and the quotation used is from a John Milton (1608–1674) sonnet.

Peace hath her victories
No less renowned than war.

Garden no. 2: Happiness

In this garden we used a simple millstone fountain, which pumped water up through the centre. The water makes a calming sound as it disperses to an underground sump. We planted a colourful selection of flowering shrubs and herbaceous plants that are associated with happiness such as lavender, lily of the valley, geraniums, honeysuckle, lupins and verbena. These are planted amongst upright standing stones of varying heights representing the various levels of happiness in our lives. The quotation is from dramatist Shackerley Marmion (1603–1639).

Great joys, like griefs, are silent.

Garden no. 3: Friendship

In this garden two flat stones are joined together on equal terms at ground level, representing true friendship. They are surrounded by Periwinkle (*Vinca*) and ivy, (*Hedera*), plants that are traditionally used to represent friendship.

The quotation, from Francis Bacon (1561–1626), reads:

Friendship

It is the worst solitude to have no true friendships.

Garden no. 4: Reconciliation

A pathway in this garden leads through a stone archway to a tranquil area that can be used as a meditative place. Here there is a group of contorted hazels (*Corylus avellana* 'Contorta') meant to represent dilemmas that need to be untwisted to reach a sense of reconciliation. The quotation here is from the Gospel of Matthew 5:24.

Go at once to make peace with your brother.

Garden no. 5: Hope

Described above.

Garden no. 6: Harmony

In this garden are three upright standing stones matched in shape and size. Planted with them are five upright mountain ash trees (*Sorbus aucuparia* 'Fastigiata').

These were chosen for their uniformity of growth and they symbolise harmony, happiness and balance – qualities that we all strive for in the autumn of our lives. The quote is from the physician and philosopher Sir Thomas Browne (1605–1682).

There is music wherever there is harmony, order or proportion.

Garden no. 7: Eternity

We created a chamber, into which we placed a time capsule containing local memorabilia, and sealed it. The time capsule contains a map of the village, a cheque book, a pension book, a list of our parish organisations and other items that we felt would be of interest when it is opened in the year 3,000. The local children participated in a ceremony in which a stone was rolled over the chamber holding the capsule. The plants used here were the guelder rose (*Viburnum opulus*) and poppies (*Papaveraceae*) representing eternity.

The quote is from the bible: Corinthians 2: 4–8.
That which cannot be seen is eternal.

The entire plot is surrounded by a bank of Cotoneaster 'Coral Beauty', a ground-covering evergreen shrub with pretty, white flowers followed by red berries. Now mature, it is a source of food and shelter for wildlife.

My friends on the Leighlinbridge improvement group often laugh about the number of 'high Nelly' bicycles and old prams we found in the thicket of poplar trees when we started on this project. To think it is now a beautiful green space supporting wildlife and providing a calming and pleasant environment in which the people of the village and visitors can stroll and contemplate makes us all very proud. We all share fond memories of the commitment of the local community and of the many friendships formed in the course of the work.

What of the competition? If you visit the Millennium Garden today, you'll see a plaque in the 'eternity' mini-garden announcing our garden as the winning Green Towns 2000 project. Yes, Leighlinbridge won the overall award and we were fêted at the prize-giving event in Dublin Castle. We got £20,000 in prize money and a taste for winning.

We didn't have long to wait for our next big community challenge to come along: the Entente Florale, a Europe-wide competition of floral display for cities, towns and villages. The competition, I discovered, was established in 1975 and run by an international committee called the Association Européenne pour le Fleurissement et le Paysage in association with the government departments responsible for agriculture and tourism in the participating countries. The aim is to raise awareness of the importance of the green environment to the quality of life in the competitor countries.

In 2001 Leighlinbridge was chosen to represent Ireland in the village category of this competition. Various Irish villages had entered the competition in previous years but none had been successful in winning a gold medal in the village category. We were determined to be the first. Our small committee worked tirelessly to this end and we had the full co-operation of Carlow County Council; everyone put in a huge effort, including the county manager and street cleaners. It was a whole-village effort. Local women worked with us and supplied tea and sandwiches, and even the children helped.

The committee persuaded the villagers to paint their houses, and for this the county council provided both a paint scheme and financial contribution. Business owners agreed to paint their establishments in subtle shades of a variety of colours. Arboretum sponsored some of the plants, and local enterprises and the county council helped with the important matter of finance and

small formal garden in Leighlinbridge opposite St. Lazerian's National School. My inspiration was Italian composer Vivaldi's famous violin concertos, The Four Seasons. The rectangular plot is divided into four quadrants. Each quadrant is surrounded by box hedging and in each there is a life-size statue representing one of the four seasons along with plants that flower in the season it represents. In the centre, where the four quadrants meet, there is a formal fountain called the Four Seasons. To carry on the musical theme, we placed musical notes made from brushed steel on the wall directly behind the garden.

The next garden, the Memorial Garden, commemorates important occasions in the history of the village, such as the visit of Brian Mulroney, Prime Minister of Canada from 1984 to 1993. He came to our village to see the birthplace of his ancestors and planted a sugar maple tree (*Acer saccharum*), the national emblem of Canada, in the garden. A liquidambar

(*Liquidambar styraciflua*) celebrates the commitment of the Sisters of Mercy to education in the village. The Memorial Arch, commemorating the Carlow men who lost their lives in the Great War (1914–1918) is also part of this garden. The Memorial Garden enjoys a beautiful location beside the River Barrow, with the towpath running past it.

The Leighlinbridge Improvement Group planted some really special trees throughout the town. Among them are Liquidamber, the Tulip Tree (*Liriodendron*), Beech (*Fagus sylvatica*) and the Maidenhair Tree (*Gingko biloba*). On either side of a pathway leading from the Parish Centre to the Church we planted the Antarctic Beech (*Notofagus antarctica*). I believe that when all these trees mature in the years to come many people will appreciate our wisdom of planting these unusual specimens.

Across the road from the Memorial Garden is the Sculpture Garden. This is dedicated to three famous

Leighlinbridge men. Each of the three men has a large limestone standing stone on which his image is embossed, and each stone has a two-metre-high semi-circular beech hedge around it. The three famous sons of Leighlinbridge are John Tyndall (1820–93), a renowned scientist, educator and physicist; Cardinal Francis Moran (1830–1911), who became the first cardinal in Australia; and Captain Myles Walter Keogh (1840–76), who fought on the Union side in the American Civil War (1861–65) and was killed alongside General Custer at the famous Battle of the Little Bighorn in 1876. My brother-in-law, the singer Richie Kavanagh, wrote a song as a tribute to our local hero:

Myles Keogh lost his life at the Little Bighorn

A long way from Carlow, the place he was born.

After the battle they were counting the dead

And when they came to Myles Keogh, the enemy said,

This man rode a horse with feathered white feet,
He was a brave man, he was hard to defeat.
His men rallied round him, they all knew the drill,
but they all died together on last stand hill.
Sitting Bull, Crazy Horse, Lakota, Cheyenne,
The great Seventh Cavalry they soon overran.

The only thing living, the only thing found,
Was Keogh's horse, Comanche, alive in the ground.
They all stepped together to the great Garryowen;
Now their memory forever is engraved in stone.

Captain Myles Keogh's memory is engraved in stone in this small, formal garden. Beside his standing stone is a single cherry tree.

Rachel's Reflection

As I planned them and our group planted and nurtured our gardens in Leighlinbridge, I realised that they would continue to enrich our community in ways I had neither planned nor envisaged.

LEAVES

Inspirational garden Leighlinbridge

Whitewater rafting

Kilquade garden centre

National Garden Exhibition Centre Kilquade and Equatorial Sundial

Arboretum delivery van with orders

Entente Floral award for best Millennium project

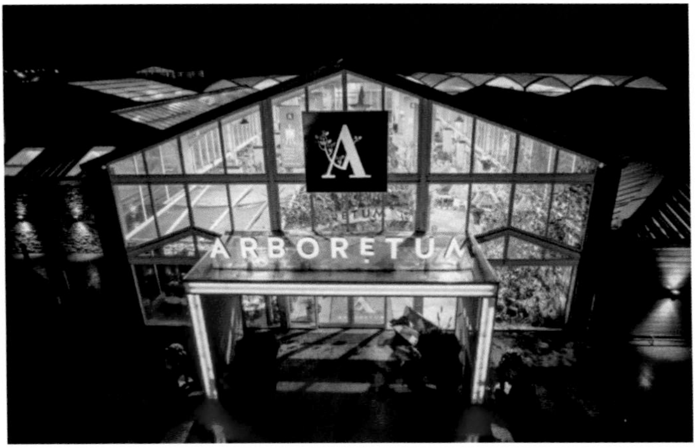

Arboretum entrance

Arboretum café

Overall winner of Green Town 2000
for Millennium project

Arboretum Leighlinbridge

Don't Rule from the Grave

The Yew (*Taxus baccata*)
This native tree was sacred to the druids.
They believed that it had qualities of longevity and regeneration. It was also believed that it guarded the doorway between this life and the next.

Just as white butterflies damage your cabbage patch every year unless you protect it with a net, there are certain questions that keep pestering you if you don't deal with them once and for all. One of those questions is that of succession. I didn't start to deal with it in earnest until 2013 but eight years earlier I was lucky enough to have had an opportunity that allowed me to at least start thinking about it.

In 2005, owing to the growing profile of Arboretum, I was invited by the television production company Tyrone Productions to take part in a programme for

RTÉ One called 'The Mentor', an eight-part series that offered a variety of Irish businesses the chance to 'make it big in the cut-throat world of corporate Ireland'. At first I was reluctant to participate, in part because I didn't see myself as being in a cut-throat corporate world, but I realised that a 30-minute slot immediately after the evening news on national television was a golden publicity opportunity for Arboretum that I couldn't refuse. So I said yes. I believe that when opportunity knocks, you should get up and open the door. Each episode of 'The Mentor' focused on a different challenge in business, and the challenge I picked was succession planning. It was a subject that'd been on my mind since my sons had become adults but one about which I felt I needed to know a little more. Tyrone Productions jumped on it, believing it would be of interest to an audience.

As the show's name suggests, the concept was that the business person to be featured in each episode would have access to a number of mentors who would help them solve the problem they were focusing on. I was fortunate to have had three incredible mentors on the show to help me: Dr Jean Bolger, the then vice-president of scientific licensing with Johnson & Johnson; Jay Bourke, who ran some of the country's most successful restaurants, bars and clubs; and the late Feargal Quinn, the well-known Senator and businessman behind Superquinn. Jay Bourke, although he urged me to get started on succession planning, rightly sensed I was nowhere near ready to hang up my boots in 2005, or perhaps ever, and that doing so would actually be detrimental to my health. His parting words were 'Don't retire.' I will never forget this. Being a workaholic, it was music to my ears. Jay's view was echoed in part by Feargal Quinn, who generously offered advice to me in private before filming.

'Don't rule from the grave,' he warned.

He made it clear that succession should happen and that it should be orderly, amicable and by agreement. But he saw a role for me after succession, namely that of ambassador for my operation. The idea excited me. Seconds later, the cameras started rolling.

In October 2005, my episode of 'The Mentor' was shown to the nation. While I was very critical of how I looked and sounded on TV, I didn't dwell on it for long. After all, the experience had sown a seed I'd wanted to sow for some time. That seed took another eight years to germinate; it wasn't something I wanted to rush.

In February 2013, Frank decided to retire from active participation in the running of the business, which he felt ready to do. I, on the other hand, was still nowhere near ready. However, we both agreed it was time to start preparing to hand over the running of the enterprise to Fergal and Barry. I won't pretend the decision to hand over wasn't immensely difficult for me but I understood the pitfalls of not making the right decision. While I had in mind Jay Bourke's advice that retirement wouldn't suit me, I was aware of businesses where the parents held onto the reins of power for too long or didn't give ownership and control to their adult children, leading to frayed emotions. I was also aware of situations where people didn't hand over and a tragedy, such as a terminal illness, intervened, resulting in an enormous loss of knowledge and know-how on top of the grief of losing a family member. When the parents' intentions aren't made clear, it is a recipe for family rifts. Our two boys had been exposed to the business since they were knee-high and had learned so much informally without even knowing it, as had I, so in my heart I knew it was time.

During the process that ensued, I kept reminding myself and my sons that every decision we were going to make would have to be based on what was ultimately best for the company. It was never ever to be about one person being better than another; it was to be about playing to our strengths and recognising our weaknesses. All of our many discussions around the boardroom table had to be respectful of everyone's opinions and feelings. It was a difficult procedure but we stuck to our guns.

To get the ball rolling I called on an individual with whom I had a great rapport, my good friend and adviser Blaise Brosnan. Blaise was someone I was always happy to bounce ideas off, and he was only too happy to come on board. Importantly, he had a keen sense of the strengths and weaknesses of both Fergal and Barry. With Blaise's help, we started doing what was required to make my sons shareholders in the company. We had a series of meetings and discussions on the subject and I benefited from this methodical approach.

Having put in train the shareholding process, I still had to decide who'd take over my job. This wasn't easy. While I had my own thoughts on it, the decision was too critical to depend on gut instinct alone. I felt it would be wise to ask the opinions of some trusted advisers.

Blaise was one of them, of course. He held one-to-one meetings with my sons to ascertain their feelings on succession, and facilitated a meeting of all the Doyles.

The other was Stratford-upon-Avon-based retail consultant Alistair Lorimer. I met Alistair originally through the English Garden Centre Association and he subsequently became a good friend and coffee companion on my trips to the UK. He was sharp with a great business brain, and I'd employed him on many occasions as an 'outside eye' to give constructive feedback on how we in Arboretum ran our operation. I used to pick him up at Dublin airport when he'd come over for these visits and I remember we once ended up in Wicklow because I was so engaged in our conversation I missed my exit on the M50! His advice was always invaluable to us and greatly appreciated by Fergal, Barry and the team. I'm sad to say he lost his battle with cancer in 2017, in his early fifties. We are still devastated by his loss. As the old saying in Irish goes, Ar dheis Dé go raibh a anam dílis. May he be seated at the right side of God.

It was on the question of whether Fergal or Barry, or both, should take on my role that I was most keen to hear Alistair's view. I wanted to know whether he'd confirm what I had in mind myself. I'd discovered that Alistair was on chemotherapy at the time, so I was reluctant to give him a call. Instead, I sent him an email saying I didn't know what stage his treatment was at but that if he was in a position to give me a ring, I'd take up only five minutes of his time. He rang as soon as he could. I was in the kitchen at the time and grabbed a notepad and biro, which I always keep beside the phone, to write down what he was going to say. After some friendly small talk, I got to the point.

'Alistair, you know my boys really well. Who do you think should be CEO, and why?

and Fergal the space they needed to establish themselves. To this day, I've never felt in any way sidelined. The boys understand my need to be kept informed!

It was actually the proudest moment of my career to have successfully completed my succession planning and have a shareholders' agreement in place.

Rachel's Reflection

I learned that courage is not the absence of fear, but the triumph over it. Nelson Mandela

Empowering the Team

Walnut (*Juglans regia*)
The walnut symbolises knowledge, growth, intelligence, abundance and wisdom. In olden times it was referred to as 'the foreign nut' because it was associated with evil and witchcraft.

As I've pointed out before, there's no standing still in business. No sooner had the succession plan been implemented than Fergal, Barry and I realised we'd some work to do on our team. As we tried to adjust to our new roles, we saw there was a major barrier to the new structure working: the day-to-day running of the business was too dependent on our family. The Leighlinbridge business had grown and we'd taken on Kilquade by this time. With all the operational demands, Fergal and Barry were just not getting the time to work at a strategic level, which is what they really needed to be doing now that they were at senior-executive level. In order to free them up from day-to-day matters, we needed to empower our managers to work more proactively and autonomously – in short, to make decisions. This would require significant delegation of responsibility on our part. It was going to be a challenge for us, the Doyle family, but we saw it was necessary.

We've always believed in developing our people and offering training to anyone wishing to improve their skills. I love the saying 'Train them, don't blame them' and I believe it too. Whenever possible, we promote from within. I gave the example of Nicole Foley, who started on the shop floor and is now our purchasing manager and head of visual merchandising. Darragh Simpson is another: he started with us as a kitchen porter in Rachel's Garden Café at Leighlinbridge and he is now supporting us on e-commerce. However, the task at hand seemed beyond our capability; we needed to develop within the team the confidence and skills our people needed to step into roles carrying more responsibility. We needed to make leaders out of them. We've always been prepared to source specific know-how when we felt we needed it, and Fergal believed he knew the right man for the job, namely Lindsay Muir of Cedar Associates.

Fergal met Lindsay at the 2017 annual conference of the UK Garden Centre Association, which was held at St. Andrews, Scotland. Lindsay had acted as a consultant in leadership training and coaching to many of our UK colleagues and his reputation preceded him. Fergal invited him to Leighlinbridge so he could see what we were about and assess whether he felt he could help us. We shared with him the many projects we were exploring, including the development of Kilquade and the Hunter's Moon property. I met him, of course, and my sons were keen to know what I thought of him, but I was all too aware that this kind of work fell straight into the remit of the chief executive officer and chief commercial officer, not that of the executive chair; in other words, I needed to stay in the background. This was a strange time for me. You can imagine how much I wanted to get stuck in. Luckily I liked Lindsay immediately and saw he knew exactly what we needed to enable Fergal and Barry to make the transition to their new roles. More than that, he liked what we were planning to achieve in the future and felt he could help us. And so we embarked on the most in-depth and structured people-development programme in our history.

It was an exciting time in the life of Arboretum, and I participated in it as fully as I felt was appropriate. I won't go into detail on the full scope of the eight-part leadership and development programme we embarked upon in 2017 but I'll give you indication of how we got started.

Under Lindsay's guiding hand, we reviewed our mission, vision and values – that trio of touchstones that keep any business on track. We explored how far away we were from achieving our development plans, or our dreams, as I'd call them. We scrutinised outside forces that could potentially influence the future development of the business; we thought about ways in which we could mitigate, avoid or capitalise on those outside forces, depending on whether they represented a threat, opportunity, strength or weakness. One of the things that had the most impact – it sounds very simple when I say it – was to really focus on our strategic objectives. How that translated into the day-to-day running of the business was that every meeting we held took on an incredible level of focus and discipline. This means we are constantly moving towards those goals instead of allowing ourselves to get side-tracked or lose interest.

Getting the views of the team members is a big part of Lindsay's approach. He started with the managers.

They were asked what our strengths were. Top of their list was that we were a family business striving for excellence at what we did. I found the fact that they picked out the family-business element for praise wonderfully heartening because the Arboretum team members are my other family. Over the years I've created a culture in which anyone in the team would feel comfortable telling us about something personal that might be affecting them, whether it's a parent with Alzheimer's or a sick child, for example, because they know we care about them. Being part of my family, they know there's an understanding between us. In the past I've told certain members of the team whom I knew were going through an exceptionally hard time that if there was an emergency at home, they were to just go, without permission or explanation. You wouldn't get that in a big corporate environment and I think the management team recognised and appreciated that as a strength.

That particular piece of feedback from the managers was positive, but some feedback was less so. One of the first things Lindsay did was survey the entire team – our team had grown to around 175 employees by this time – on how they felt we were doing. He referred to it as a colleague survey. This would be an anonymous survey, giving the respondents complete freedom to say what they wanted. I couldn't wait to read the responses. I remember taking a deep breath before I opened the report on the survey results Lindsay had compiled. Though I was a little bit apprehensive, I felt that whatever the results were, we'd work with them and improve our performance. I firmly believe it's good to be challenged. Well, I can tell you I was challenged when I read that the team didn't think we were doing a good job of communicating with them, something I considered us good at! Specifically, they thought we could be better at telling them about projects or developments that were coming down the track. It's natural that they should want to know about those sorts of projects because they'd want reassurance that their futures would be secure, but it hadn't occurred to me before the colleague survey revealed it. This led us to become more disciplined about meetings and how information is passed from managers to their teams, and we now make sure to share updates on future projects.

Listening to the team is important in any business and when you show you're taking their opinions seriously, the reward is enormous. A little over half the employees completed the first colleague survey in 2017. When we repeated it in late 2021 as part of the final tranche of work with Cedar Associates, we were very pleased to get 100 percent participation. I believe the improvement was down to the team members feeling they'd been listened to. This had the effect of making them feel they had ownership of issues they'd brought to our attention in the survey. It really was such a worthwhile exercise. We are committed to repeating the colleague survey regularly. Not only does it work wonders for team engagement but it also helps us enormously as a business. The survey responses brought issues to our attention that we weren't even aware of. Our team members, because they are on the ground, notice things that we do not, and the colleague survey allows us to tap into that knowledge

I absolutely loved the work we were doing with Lindsay, but not everybody did. We realized we needed to create new roles, an operations manager and purchasing manager. Some team members found the change challenging and we had some resignations. This was what we predicted and I believe, was a good outcome because the process had shown them that they had gone as far as they wanted to with us and it was time to leave. That was good for them and good for us. The price of doing the same old thing is far greater than the price of change.

For some time Fergal had been convinced of the value of having a non-executive director to sit on our board. Looking back, I can say I probably dragged my heels on this one. For us to appoint a non-family member to our board was a major decision. I probably became convinced of the value of it only when we finally found the right person. It took a while. We talked to a number of people but none ticked all the boxes until we landed on Kevin Neary. Fergal and Barry had previously met him on a retail trip to New York and I'd met him through the good offices of Retail Excellence Ireland. I'd had a strong, positive gut reaction to him the minute I met him. There are so many ways in which he adds to the business – his acumen, his calm disposition and his ability to relate to people, to give just some examples. He adds a whole new dimension to our enterprise and yet is the perfect match for us. He brings that outside perspective to the table, which is exactly what Fergal believed we needed. He's brought structure and discipline to the workings of our board and we've made much progress on our vision for the future. We're privileged to have him on our team and look forward to his visits.

Having taken what I'd describe as a leap of faith in including a board member from outside the family, Lindsay wanted us to take another. As I said earlier, we all knew Fergal and Barry needed to spend more of their time working on strategy but Lindsay put a figure on it. He said they should be working on strategic matters 60 percent of the time. While developing the team to take more responsibility was going to be important in their ability to achieve this, it wasn't going to be enough. We soon accepted that a new role would have to be created, that of operations manager. And so began a long search for the right person. Eventually, we found him – Barry Gardner.

Hiring Barry turned out to be a game-changer for Arboretum. He has a retail background and he instantly bought into our ethos and values. When we interviewed him for the position, I instantly thought he was right for the job. Our directors were of the same mind and three years later we haven't changed that opinion. I recall a description of a manager that impressed me: a manager needs to stretch his or her team to help them to achieve their full potential, and one of the most powerful ways to do this is by saying 'I believe in you.' These four words can be the most inspirational message a manager can give. Barry is that kind of manager.

Working on the business is a constant necessity. As I write, Lindsay Muir, along with Barry Gardner, is delivering a bespoke training programme, which we've called the Arboretum Academy. The aim of this is to equip our managers to deliver training to new and existing team members on the five values that underpin our business as well as other training that was identified in the recent colleague survey. There is also an internally certified eight-module management development programme designed to empower our managers to develop and lead their teams effectively. The idea behind this is to make in-house coaches of our managers. It's refreshing to see how enthusiastic our team are about change and the future.

We've been presented with new challenges – Brexit, COVID-19, rising fuel costs, the move to online shopping and the increase in our workforce – but with people like Kevin Neary and Lindsay on our side, we feel as equipped as any SME to meet them head-on. In fact, as I write, we are deep in preparations for the opening of Arboretum Urban Green, a Dublin city-centre outlet. My son Barry has been burning the midnight oil to research new products, product categories and the optimal store layout including where best to locate the café. This is all made possible by Barry's wife Lynda keeping all the activities of their three young boys going. Fergal and Barry have a very clear shared vision. Just like me all those years ago, they are following their dreams.

At a time when corporate governance is taking on greater significance, I am proud to say that Fergal is on his way to becoming a chartered director with the Institute of Directors. This reassures me even more that Arboretum will weather whatever storms are on the horizon. I'm so proud of my sons and the team they have assembled. Exciting times ahead.

Rachel's Reflection

As our team grows, so does the necessity for clear structures, guidelines and procedures. People who have a positive attitude and are totally committed to our five pillars are worth their weight in gold.

A People Business

Maidenhair Tree (*Ginkgo biloba*)
This tree is the symbol of strength, hope and peace.
It has existed for over 200 million years.
It is considered to be a living fossil. Its common
name relates to the similarity between
the leaves and that of the maidenhair fern.

Someone once remarked that I don't use the word 'leader' about myself. That really stopped me in my tracks because it's true, and yet, looking back on my career, I have always led by example. I remember walking through Arboretum one day with Fergal in the early days of his involvement in the business. He was trying to tell me something important but he wasn't getting very far because I kept stopping to chat to customers. 'Do you have to say hello to everyone?' he joked. 'Yes, I do,' I replied, 'and so should you. These are the people who pay our wages.' This is now a culture we have created throughout the Arboretum team.

Retail is a people business. I believe that those of us who are in retail need to be single-minded in our quest to deliver first-class, well-planned customer service so that the people we serve love what we do, stay loyal to our brand and keep us in business. I never cease to remind myself and others that at Arboretum the majority of the products we sell are not essential; customers come to us to spend discretionary money, so we must work especially hard. When it comes to customer service I believe in the saying, 'Being good is not good enough'; we must excel. I am very conscious and observant of good and bad customer service everywhere I go. I am shocked at how many people in the service industry cannot smile and don't know the words 'Please' and 'Thank you', not to mention 'Hello'. I have techniques to help me remember people's names.

I associate the name with a flower, someone I know or someone I feel has a resemblance to the person. Customers love it when we address them by name.

Offering really excellent customer service is as important a part of Arboretum as I am. I'm often asked how we do it. In the early days it was easier as we were a small team. We hired great people who shared our values. I mentioned before that I hire for attitude because the rest we can teach. Frank and I were in the business every day, leading by example. But when the business experienced rapid growth after our move to Leighlinbridge, and even more so when we acquired Kilquade, we simply could not rely on people having the opportunity to work alongside Fergal, Barry or me in order to understand how we wanted them to behave. We had to find another way to transmit our values.

When Lindsay Muir started working with us in 2017 we attempted to capture those values in a booklet that would be part of every team member's induction.

Rather than calling them values, we called them 'pillars' because, without them, the business could collapse. Customer service is one of them, of course, and the others are communication, commitment, reputation and leadership.

Customer Service is respecting customers and creating a great shopping experience. It is the little things like smiling, saying hello, remembering names and product preferences, but also the big things like knowing the stock and dealing with complaints effectively. I believe in dealing with complaints immediately – 'nipping it in the bud', to use a horticultural term. When dealing with complaints in Arboretum, our goal is to turn a negative situation into a positive one. I recall an occasion that illustrates this in action. A lady brought two Japanese azaleas to Eamonn Wall, our outdoor manager. Both plants were dead. Eamonn explained that they had died because they were not watered and had dried out. He gave her two new azaleas and instructed her on how to care for them. He then drew her attention to the fact that she hadn't bought them from us (the original label was still on the plant). She came back to Arboretum a few days later, sought me out and told me of the wonderful service she had received from Eamonn. She is now a customer for life and a great advocate for our business.

Communication is the next pillar. Communication is a two-way thing, as we learned from the colleague survey. As a business, our contract with our team members is that we will inform them about the business and give them regular feedback on how they are carrying out their roles to enable them to be accountable. In turn, we will listen to them. Communication also relates to how our team members deal with customers on a face-to-face basis – I often remind the team that our interaction with a customer could be his or her only conversation with another human being that day – and how we as a brand communicate via digital or other means with our existing and potential customers.

Commitment, in the Arboretum sense, is a willingness to work hard and to learn. It is also about being committed to colleagues, our customers and the company by being honest, respectful and loyal.

We trade on our reputation and it is important that we are all aware of how fragile it is and that we do our utmost to uphold it. Our reputation rests on customer service, of course, but also on the quality of the products we sell and the way we sell them. We are known as a forward-looking and outwardly focused family business, and to uphold that reputation we must continue to bring our customers newness and innovation in the retail environment. That refers to online as well as in-store. We are firmly in the age of digital technology and we have to embrace it. People now research on their phones, order online and have access to businesses across the globe. We have to adapt to and understand these technologies and we have to be innovative in everything we do in this new world.

Leadership completes our five pillars. Through leadership we achieve high standards and positive results while developing and motivating people to work effectively and efficiently. I mentioned in the last chapter that since 2017 we have been undertaking a comprehensive leadership development programme for our managers with the help of Lindsay Muir. This is certainly not a 'nice to have'. In a business our size it is a 'must have'.

The five pillars booklet is an important part of every team member's induction process. We also give them a copy of a book called *You Are the Difference*, written by our good friend Alf Dunbar. The book, and indeed the customer service coaching programme that inspired it, which Alf has delivered many times for us, touches on the principles I feel are essential in retail.

The emphasis on our values is not confined to the induction process. We champion it every day. Each week, at the Friday morning team meeting, we give a 'Surprise and Delight' reward to a team member who has gone over and above in carrying out their duties. We use mystery shopper visits, carried out by a market research company several times a year, as a barometer of how we are doing. The mystery shopper arrives unannounced and starts the evaluation from the entrance gate. He or she progresses through the carpark, then goes into the store and through every department and finally makes a transaction at the till. The marking is weighted heavily on customer service, including friendliness, eye contact, smiles and how knowledgeable the team members are. The mystery shopper interacts with a number of different team members, all of whom wear nametags and are easily identified. He or she will also telephone with a query and mark us on how long the phone rings before it is answered and how well the query is responded to. We find the mystery shopper visits a very effective tool for keeping us on track, and we always share the findings with the team so that it is a learning experience for all of us.

Our relationship with our customers extends beyond selling goods in our shops or food in our cafes; that is something I have always understood. The events we run, such as gardening masterclasses, fashion shows, Weber barbecue demonstrations not to mention our renowned Santa experiences, are opportunities for us to express our values. We usually host the opening or closing event in the annual Carlow Garden Festival, which takes place at the end of July each year and is organised with great gusto by Carlow Tourism. Our most popular speaker ever has been Monty Don of the BBC's *Gardeners' World* programme. We've had many accomplished gardeners speak at Arboretum but Monty's style of delivery and knowledge are second to none. In 2022, after the COVID-19 hiatus, we were delighted to host a 'design-off' between celebrity gardeners Adam Frost and James Alexander Sinclair. It really was lovely to have the festival back and to be able to welcome so many avid gardeners once again to Arboretum in Leighlinbridge. Because of the popularity of these two Gardeners' World celebrities we will have them back in 2023 and hope to have Monty Don in 2024. We clear all the benches out of the atrium for these events in order to accommodate 800 seats. It's a huge amount of work for the team, which must be carried out after business hours, but nobody complains. We approach all our events with the same desire to be better than good that we apply to the everyday activity of the business.

In recent years we've started holding events for our team members as well. The annual team awards night, for example, is a glitzy affair in a different local hotel each year. We go the whole hog; partners are invited, there's banquet, dancing into the night and a motivational speaker. We've had Blaise Brosnan; the hurling manager and Ireland's Fittest Family coach Davy Fitzgerald; the former managing director of Hamilton Osborne King and motivational speaker Paul McNeive; the former Munster and Ireland rugby player John 'The Bull' Hayes; and the CEO of HaloCare and former CEO of Netwatch, David Walsh. We consider this award ceremony to be money well spent. It's our way of recognising the hard work and dedication of each and every Arboretum team member but we also present a number of awards, culminating in the Employee of the Year award. These awards champion the individuals who embody our pillars in a remarkable way and what's really special about them is that the winners are chosen by their colleagues. The coronavirus pandemic forced us to pause the team awards night but we were delighted that in March 2023 we had our awards in our local hotel The Lord Bagenal with our international speaker Rory O'Connor of Rory's Stories fame.

Our in-house awards are a relatively new thing, but, as you know, we are no strangers to industry awards programmes. From early in our history I have felt it was important to put ourselves forward for industry awards and I really do love winning them for two very powerful reasons: winning brings recognition to our team for the hard work they put in day after day, and it makes us more determined than ever to maintain and raise our standards.

I glossed over the part that recruitment plays in upholding our values. There's a saying in business that springs to mind: we don't hire people and train them to be nice; we hire nice people. However, you can come across nice people who do a great interview. Once in the job, though, you can find that they're not the right fit – they don't share our values. It's not that they're bad people; it's just that they would be more suited to working somewhere else. This has happened surprisingly few times in my career because I have a sixth sense when it comes to people. What I mean by that is I have a very strong gut reaction to people. In the early days, I did all the hiring myself and I still like to conduct the second interview. I don't always manage to, however. I recall a staff member appearing in the business whom I had not met. I couldn't help feeling that something was not right. I had a look at her CV and saw she'd worked in a local business. I asked her line manager if her references had been checked. She assured me they had. However, I knew the owner of the business she'd worked for most recently and I contacted him. It turned out he'd sacked her for stealing. She had given a friend's mobile number as the referee's contact number and naturally he'd given her a glowing reference when our manager called. My sixth sense has been proved right more than once, so I don't ignore it.

I am happy to say that, on the whole, our team members are fabulous people. I love meeting our former employees, who often have warm memories of their time here. I had a call recently from a former employee who was looking for advice on whether or not he should do a doctorate in horticulture. He had worked with us ten years previously and, since leaving us, had done a degree in agriculture and worked abroad. We met for a coffee and talked for about two hours, during which time he told me about all the things he'd learned here at Arboretum that he'd brought with him. It meant the world to me that what he'd learned from us had helped him in his career and in his life. It shows we're doing something right in the way we develop our people. Needless to say I told him to do the doctorate. 'If you wanted someone to put you off, you came to the wrong person!' I said.

Let me come back to the question of how we do it, of how we give great customer service and how we demonstrate all our values every day. In each case the answer is that we do it through hard work. By making it a focus we make it happen. As you know by now, I myself am a course junkie, so it will come as no surprise to you that training is a big part of how we do it. Training must be continuous; one or two courses now and again are not enough to create a culture and to ensure that all the team members understand the ethos of the company. I'm delighted with the training and development that Lindsay has been doing with us and I can see the results in enthusiasm and engagement as well as confidence and competence.

I now see that our pillars are our brand. This was not always the case! I used to believe that branding was a logo. We had a nice logo and therefore I assumed we had a nice brand. To me, a brand was just a visual cue that was shorthand for our name. Around 1997 I had come across the phrase 'Put your brand value on your balance sheet'; in other words, the trust and confidence that your brand represents could have a monetary value to the business. I decided we could improve on our logo.

While the word 'Arboretum' has always been in our branding, there have been various logos and naming styles throughout the years. New logos tended to emerge from major revamps. We developed our 'blue' logo around 2004–05, when we carried out our first big revamp of the Leighlinbridge site – this was when we created our glass atrium. 'Arboretum Lifestyle and Garden Centre' in white font, all lower case letters, sat on a vibrant blue background, with a green curve, not unlike a blade of grass, stretching from the 'b' to the 'm'. I don't quite remember how it came about but it certainly wasn't the result of a design process involving brand consultants or designers! More likely it was sketched out in the office and refined by a graphic designer. It was cheerful and vibrant and we put no more thought into it than that.

Our current logo emerged out of the 2014 refit, in which we added Rachel's Garden Café and the covered plant area. Builders were on site, gutting the shop, and Fergal, Barry and myself were catching up with our interior architect, Barry McCabe. 'Now might be a good time to look at your brand', he suggested. 'It's a golden opportunity to start afresh, come up with something really meaningful.' We had not intended to revamp the logo as well, yet none of us disagreed with him and we were soon in the hands of Tom Meenaghan, an award-winning designer and creative director. Where we did disagree was on the need to include a descriptive line in the design, like 'lifestyle and garden centre'. We sat around the table with Tom some weeks later in the unfinished café arguing over and back. Fergal and Barry felt the name Arboretum was well enough known and a strong enough brand proposition not to need any explanation. Tom finally threw out a suggestion that would put an end to the debate: 'Ask your customers,' he said. And so we did. We conducted a survey, the results of which confirmed that the name Arboretum was indeed strong enough to stand on its own.

Tom designed a beautiful letter A in an art deco font with the stem of the A as a branch bearing leaves. In addition to the A, he produced the full word Arboretum in the art deco font and style and has over the years expertly applied the branding to all manner of things from signage to digital platforms such as our website and our new app to packaging for our own-brand products. Tom continues to provide us with design solutions for the business. We use the words 'Home and Garden Heaven' here and there where we feel they are needed, but they're not part of the logotype.

I now understand that the logo is just one part of what makes up a brand. Our brand is a promise to our customers of the buying experience they will have but also of the relationship we, the business, will have with them. Branding is not about product; it is about our values. As the embodiment of our values, our people are also our brand. On the back of the Arboretum uniform, there's a large A. It is intended to stand for 'Ask', but to me it means 'The A Team' – in other words, the best people for the job.

As you might expect, we carried our branding and values through to our customer loyalty programme, A-List, which we launched in 2015. It is special as loyalty programmes go in that it isn't a points-collecting programme; instead, we offer our customers benefits, rewards and surprises based on their purchasing behaviour. We give several spend-driver rewards throughout the year whereby an A-List member gets an item that has a perceived high value for them for free when they spend a certain amount in-store in one transaction in a particular month. Our rose spend-driver is very successful – some customers come back another time and get a second rose. We have been known to run out of roses long before the end of the month. The roses are contract grown for us, so it isn't a matter of simply ordering more. Early in the year we have a big decision to make as to how many to order. In business there is value in creating a sense of scarcity, but we don't want to disappoint our customers either. There is a balance to be struck.

The spend-drivers require action on the member's part but our members get rewards like a slice of birthday cake during their birth month, and every tenth hot drink free without having to do anything. We call them 'Just Because' rewards. We also do 'Random Acts of Kindness' every now and again. This could be handing out coffee-and-cake vouchers on a random day. On entering the store (or the Arboretum website or app), A-List members see signs displaying A-List-only prices or multi-buy offers. This underlines the feeling that they are in an exclusive club in which they get special treatment, which they do – we open sales early for them and open booking for events including our popular

Santa experiences before we open to the general public. As a result of this special treatment, our A-List members feel valued. This is good for our business in so many ways, one of them being an increased average transaction value (ATV) when A-List members shop with us. Our substantial database of members is a 'hot' audience for us – in other words, they want to hear from us. We use the mailing list strategically; our emails to A-List members communicate an exclusive A-List offer, share news about the business, or useful information about gardening or the product ranges we supply. Our open rates often touch on 60 percent, which is exceptional, and our unsubscribe rates are extremely low. I could write a whole book on how valuable A-List is to our business, but the point I really want to make is that A-List works for us because it's built on our five pillars: customer service, communication, commitment, reputation and leadership.

Having given away some key insights into our business, in the next chapter, I'll spill even more secrets.

Rachel's Reflection

It takes as much time to be average as to be excellent.

The Secrets of My Success

Holly (*Ilex aquifolium*)

In Celtic mythology the holly represents peace and goodwill. It is a source of food and shelter for the birds. In spring its fragrant white flowers are loved by butterflies and bees. Holly is also known as the 'Tree of Sacrifice'.

I recently found the results of a personality test I did in 1998. It said I was a kind-hearted and considerate person and that, because of this, people might think I was a soft touch; they would be wrong, it said, for I was not someone who would give in easily. This analysis was probably not what you might call scientifically robust, but I think it is spot on. This combination of kindness and steel is, I believe, one of the things that made me successful in business. When you're running a business the size and scale of Arboretum, you have to make hard decisions, including, occasionally, letting people go. I have rarely had to sack anyone but I always found it difficult. I recall one occasion when I was considering sacking someone who had been stealing from us. I had been on the phone getting advice from a human resources consultant. The walls were paper thin at the time and when I came out of my office, a colleague, perhaps seeing the look on my face, was prompted to say, ‘Rachel, I just want to say to you that we all think you’re firm but fair.’ It was just what I needed to hear at that moment because, naturally, I felt awful about having to fire the man, even though he was being dishonest.

In writing this book, I have been forced to think about what exactly contributed to the success of the business. Being firm but fair is one of the factors. I am delighted to learn that Arboretum is in the top five best employers, announced by Retail Excellence Ireland in 2023. We set out to be a good employer; we give our employees all the opportunities we can afford to give them. We create an environment that inspires team engagement. It makes me very proud to have been assessed by an outside party and considered one of the best retail employers in the country.

In the last chapter, I covered how important it is to have amazing and wonderful people working with us. The trouble we take to make sure they understand and share our ethos is also significant. To me it is a given, but I must accept that not every business owner places such store in these things. I will therefore chalk it up as a differentiating factor that has worked to our advantage. My sons are just as committed to this as I have been, so I know it will continue to be a feature of the Arboretum way.

The ability to make good decisions in business goes without saying. I believe that opportunities have to be realised in the lifetime of the opportunity. The opportunity could have gone by the time some people make a decision. That is not me. I see things as black or white, right or wrong. I have described myself as someone who takes calculated risks. By that I mean I think deeply about the decision to be made, pray about it, listen to others' viewpoints, make a list of the pros and cons, and then make my determination. When I've made my decision, I don't look back. I go for it with all the passion and energy I have.

I think location has been instrumental in our success. Experts looking on might say that we set ourselves up for failure – twice! Yet I don't regret any of our decisions on that score: starting the business at my home as I got the enterprise off the ground was the right thing for me; moving to Carlow made sense once the business was established; and purchasing our own site in 1986 was the logical thing to do because it turned dead money (rent) into an asset, which turned out to be very valuable. Yes, moving back to Leighlinbridge in 2000 when we'd sold our Carlow site to Aldi was a risk, but it paid off and we've been able to expand several times on the site, something we wouldn't have been able to do had we stayed in Carlow.

Without a doubt, my belief in the importance of having a food offering has been a significant factor in our success. In the mid-1980s, when we built our first purpose-built garden centre in Carlow, a café in a garden centre was unheard of, at least in Ireland, yet I felt it would be good for footfall. I learned from that experience that in order to be in full control of the business reputation, it is better to be in control of the food offering too. We devoted a large amount of floor space in the first iteration of Arboretum Leighlinbridge to what would be Mulberry's Restaurant, and each time we expanded in the first two decades of the new millennium, the food and beverage part of our business expanded too. My belief in the ability of really good food, cooked in-house, to attract footfall to the Leighlinbridge store – and now also Kilquade – has been proved right, not least by the many awards we have won for it.

I joined the IGCA in 1995. As you know, I never missed an annual Congress. Those trips gave me the opportunity to see the very best garden centres and horticulture businesses in the world. This made us outward looking as a business. We'd see innovative approaches on our travels and be the first to try them out in Ireland. We networked. We learned from the top people in our industry; many of them became friends. The advice and help we've received from them have been incredibly beneficial to us. I believe our membership and how we maximised it made us a leader among garden centres in Ireland. I am thrilled that Fergal and Barry are carrying on the tradition and are as active in the IGCA as I was (and still am, having just returned, with Fergal and Barry, from a superb Congress in The Netherlands).

Know your customer – it's a basic tenet of retail. From the widowed pensioner to the billionaire and from the farmer to the millennial mum, we have to know and understand them all. Today there are many software tools available to help us understand our customers but there is nothing like simply being on the shop floor. I believe it's so important to listen to the team because they are listening to the customer.

I have always kept a close eye on the spreadsheets. It's just possible that this tendency comes from having done accountancy for my leaving cert, but it's more likely that it comes from hearing my dad say 'Cut your cloth according to your measure' many times growing up. It was one of his favourite sayings. In all seriousness, cash flow is the lifeblood of business. We must pay our bills and pay them on time. I highly value having a first-class credit rating. We purchase stock, apply our margins, sell at a competitive price and pay our taxes, non-payment of which, I believe, is both criminal and immoral.

The COVID-19 pandemic that struck the world in 2020 totally changed things for our business. We had to be agile and innovative, more so than at any other time in our history. I'll give you just a couple of examples to illustrate how we reacted to what was an existential threat to Arboretum.

We saw the popularity of gardening go through the roof during the pandemic as people were confined to their homes and began to appreciate the value of having a pleasant outdoor space. I've always believed in the role gardening plays in good mental health and during those difficult months of lockdown it seemed that everyone suddenly became switched on to this truth. We were anxious to reach out to these people, these first-time or improver gardeners; yet, our stores were closed, or open in a very limited way. We had so much knowledge to share and while we couldn't host our usual in-person masterclasses, we could do what the whole world was doing – go virtual. We made use of the 'Live' function on the social media platform Instagram. This enabled us to film one of our horticulturists giving a class and to stream it live to everyone on Instagram who chose to watch us. We did these half-hour masterclasses roughly once a month and more often during the peak gardening season. We covered all manner of topics of interest to the novice gardener while making sure there was something for the more experienced gardener to learn: grow your own veg, planting potatoes, houseplants, spring bulbs, summer bulbs, lawn care, ponds and hydrangeas, to name but a few. We were able to capitalise on the huge following Arboretum had attracted on the social media platforms Instagram and Facebook. This was something Fergal had worked hard on since taking on his chief commercial officer role and it was paying off.

Our live online masterclasses reached far more people than our in-person ones ever could. Viewers were even able to ask questions, just as they might at an in-person masterclass: they could send questions in advance by way of a 'question box' feature on Instagram and they could also send questions in while the lessons were happening. These would be relayed to the horticulturist and answered. Because our online shop was geared up – another of Fergal's projects – we were able to sell the items we talked about in the virtual lessons. They have proved so successful in terms of branding, online sales and footfall that we have continued with the format even after all the COVID-19 restrictions were lifted.

We have had an online shop since 2010, but in 2017, when Fergal became chief commercial officer, we decided to invest more in this critical channel to the market. This was something I hadn't previously embraced and wasn't convinced would work for our business. At heart, I'm still a 'bricks-and-mortar' shopper who enjoys experiencing products with all my senses but I realise how much the consumer has changed; however, when it came to selling plants, the horticulturist in me was not persuaded. I recall a conversation with Fergal.

'Whatever about a trowel or grass seed, people will never buy trees or plants online,' I told him.

'Mam, not everyone needs to touch and feel a plant before they buy it,' he replied with absolute conviction. I remained dubious.

Shortly after that we sold ten trees via the website to a housing estate in Carlow and a large number of pots to an architect in Dublin. I was converted.

During the pandemic our online shop really came into its own. We even sourced special packaging so that we could ship cold-sensitive houseplants. I have always been a fan of the houseplant and we have long devoted a large area just before the tills to houseplants in our

Leighlinbridge store so that our customers exit through plants. During the pandemic, the popularity of houseplants rocketed and rightly so. I always consider plants to be the lungs of the earth. Plants absorb CO_2 and convert it to oxygen, which we all need to live and breathe. A key characteristic of many houseplants, which came to the fore during this time, was their ability to eliminate up to 87% of the dangerous toxins in the air. They can do this in 24 hours. Plants can also help to reduce stress, and improve our moods and our productivity – exactly what many of us wanted and needed as our lives were upended and we tried not to feel anxious about everything. Even before houseplants became an Instagram sensation, I saw them as oxygen machines that we should all have in our homes and in our offices. They are not only beautiful but also beneficial to our well-being. They attracted a new, younger customer to Arboretum because you don't even need a garden or a balcony to have a houseplant.

Online sales of houseplants, seeds, compost, tools and in fact anything related to gardening kept the business going in those dark days of 2020 and 2021. From fifty orders a week, we went to 150 orders a day and more. I remember being in the warehouse in the early days, marvelling at the address labels going on the packages – they were going to all thirty-two counties. We ended up having to deploy a separate building as a fulfilment centre for our online shop. The fulfilment centre has its own team and is now a stand-alone business with a logistics manager heading it up.

That our customers are everywhere in the country now is thanks to our ability to react quickly to changes in the marketplace, but it is also down to the work we started with Lindsay Muir in 2017. He led us in 'future thinking', trying to predict what could be on the horizon in the next five years. We didn't predict a global pandemic, of course, but we anticipated the move to online shopping and were therefore ready to trade online when that was the only way to trade. At times of unprecedented change new opportunities present themselves and out of bad comes good. 'Necessity is the mother of invention,' as my father used to say. I firmly believe that it is not what happens but how we meet the obstacles put in front of us and find a way to work around them that counts. We have faced adversity in the business before – the flooding of our Carlow premises, the recession of 2008, the M9 motorway bypassing our business – but we acted fast and took control of the situation in each case. I believe we are the gatekeepers of our own destiny and that if we have courage, commitment, passion and a 'can do' attitude, we will succeed.

On the subject of adapting to change, in 2022 we just decided to put on hold our plans for expanding Kilquade and developing Hunter's Moon. This was due to the rapid rise in the cost of construction. It was hugely disappointing, but it's a good example of cutting our cloth according to the measure. We aim to proceed with this huge project starting in August 2023. We plan to create a net-zero-emissions building. On my recent trip to the Netherlands for the IGCA Congress, I saw how far behind we are in this country when it comes to sustainability. Though we are already taking many steps as a business towards meeting sustainability goals, Fergal, Barry and I came back from the trip inspired to redouble our efforts. We must respond immediately to the crisis facing the climate. I am a firm believer in having a plan. No project, big or small, should be undertaken without a plan, and we have a comprehensive plan in place for this big task ahead. While the outlook for the planet is bleak, particularly if we don't all make significant changes immediately, I am positive by nature. I look at it this way: problems are opportunities turned inside out. Perhaps that is another secret of my success.

Rachel's Reflection

Trials have no value or intrinsic meaning in themselves. It's the way we respond to those trials that makes all the difference. Joni Eareckson Tada

The Ambassador's Brief

Indian Bean Tree (*Catalpa bignonioides*)

A native of North America, the West Indies and East Asia, the bean tree symbolises the promise that a dry seed, given the right care, will grow into a tree. The bark, leaves and seed were said to have medicinal purposes.

In business, as in a garden, the weather changes from one day to the next, with days of sunshine giving way to unexpected storms. The seasons change too, of course, and a time eventually arrives when you realise the saplings you have nurtured and staked against the wind are now strong enough to survive on their own and give pleasure to a new generation. Having turned seventy recently, I fulfilled another of my dreams. I treated Frank and myself to an amazing trip on the Orient Express starting in Venice traveling through five countries and finishing up in my favourite city Paris. I have taken a little step back and I watch with pride as Fergal and Barry make the major business decisions and, I am glad to say, hold to the principles I held to down the years. I act primarily in an advisory role. My sons highly value my opinions, guidance and input and refer to me as the 'Arboretum ambassador', a title I'm more than happy to accept. There's no way I'd be able to step back completely. Every morning I walk up the path from my house to Arboretum, anxious just to be there and interact with the customers and the team. Arboretum has been my life, after all. Sandra Byrne, a dear colleague who worked beside me in our office years ago, once said to me with a laugh, 'You know, Rachel, you have three children: Fergal, Barry and Arboretum.'

Thankfully, my life today is far less stressful than when my business was just a tiny green shoot requiring all my attention – those crazy times when I got up at four in the morning to bake cakes, coconut buns and scones for the café before opening the garden centre for a full day's work at nine. And that was on top of running a landscaping business on the side and the not-insignificant matter of rearing two boys. Having said that, doing nothing is not in my DNA and I always lead a hectic life. As I write, I notice that my desk is piled high with documents to be read on Westport House. I have been appointed a non-executive director of the historic house in 400 acres of parkland and am giving it my all. I am so excited about the progress and development of this amazing world class project and feel privileged to work with the Hughes family and the board.

I have already mentioned that, in the height of my career, I was involved with various community bodies and projects dedicated to the common good. It is no less true now than it was then. There's no need for me to elaborate on all the organisations I am connected with today, save to say that being involved with them gives me great personal satisfaction. I hope it goes beyond the personal, however, and that my efforts will do some good.

When the COVID-19 pandemic hit in March 2020, the manager of the Local Enterprise Office, Kieran Comerford, contacted me and my good friend David Walsh, former CEO of Netwatch and now CEO of HaloCare, to ask both of us if we would organise a mentoring scheme for young business people in Carlow. I jumped at the opportunity. David and I each asked seven business friends to help and we each committed to volunteer ten hours of our time to mentor selected companies. I believe it is good to give something of our experience and success back to society; indeed, it is a duty.

I have become a member of the diocesan financial committee for the Diocese of Kildare and Leighlin, together with Bishop Denis Nulty and a number of diocesan clergy and lay people. I am delighted to be part of this team and find the committee work interesting.

Maybe it's not by chance that I'm on the diocesan committee. My faith has always been a deep consolation to me and I try to live it every day. Faith is a personal thing that many people don't discuss; however, because of its importance to my life and my belief in having a strong moral compass in business, I want to express my feelings on it. I was raised in a very Catholic home where the Rosary was said every night and where, when the bell tolled on the radio for the Angelus, everybody stopped to recite it aloud. Attending Sunday Mass is still very much part of my week and gives meaning and structure to my busy life. It keeps me grounded. When making business decisions throughout my career, regardless of whether those decisions were big or small, I always said a prayer for guidance. I have always trusted an inner voice or sixth sense and my trust in God has never let me down. When travelling, I attend Sunday Mass if at all possible, even if it is in an unfamiliar language. As for what comes after this life, the best way to explain what I believe is to draw an analogy between it and my electric car. When in self-drive mode, my car senses when I'm approaching another vehicle and slows down to a stop, without me doing anything. It's mysterious and amazing. I trust there will be an afterlife just as I trust my electric car will stop, even though I don't fully understand how it works. When I go to my hereafter, I will ask God to put a project on my desk to keep me busy. Would there be any bliss in Heaven without that?

When my Dad went to his hereafter suddenly in 1980, I was very annoyed that God had taken such an incredibly wonderful, gifted person. Soon after that, during the beet-harvesting season, I was out driving and nearly smashed into the back of a lorry on its way to the beet factory in Carlow. I managed to slam on my brakes just in time and when I eventually skidded to a halt, the back of the lorry's trailer was just inches from my windscreen.

'Thank you, Dad,' I whispered.

I had been thinking of Dad and believe he protected me.

I would love it if Dad and Mam could see Arboretum today as I have always believed they have been with me on my journey. I often wonder what they would make of the world I live in today. Although they might be perplexed, and perhaps dismayed, I hope they'd be proud of what I've become and recognise that I at least try to keep the flame of their values alive. While people now interact on their phones, shop and bank online, and have access to millions of people and businesses across the globe, I'm convinced that the fundamental human values of face-to-face contact, character and integrity are as crucial as ever in both life and business, if not more so. 'If you haven't your character, you have nothing,' my parents used to say, and they were not wrong.

Character is not all that is required in business, of course; there is much more. In the preceding chapter I shared some of the things I believe were instrumental in my success in business, but I cannot stress enough the importance of being completely driven and brave in pursuing the goals you set for yourself. If you are starting out in business, pursuing them will involve making many mistakes, just as I made many in most facets of my venture, from franchising and customer flow to time management and recruitment. You just have to learn from these mistakes, dust yourself down and continue doing the best you can. If you are to take on board just one thing from my story about Arboretum, I hope it is this: although we should follow our dreams, they don't come true just because we wish them to; they must be wrestled into reality.

Business nowadays can be competitive and tough, so the perseverance and competence needed must be accompanied by passion and self-belief. My sons Fergal and Barry, when they were young boys doing their primary-school homework at the kitchen table, would frequently say 'I can't do it', and I would always respond with 'You're right, but if you say you *can* do it, you're also right.' I think they understood. I left primary school feeling undereducated, inadequate and self-effacing. It took me years to be able to say 'I can do it', but say it I eventually did. I still have butterflies in my stomach before making speeches and presentations, but, while I am well aware of my own shortcomings, I will never allow anyone to put me down.

Nowadays people often ask me what motivates me in business. Indeed, it's a question I frequently ask myself. If I were pushed to answer, I'd say I'm motivated by success. Where there is success, financial gain follows.

To be successful, it definitely helps to do something you love doing, and if that isn't immediately possible you should do what you have to do until you can do what you love to do. I believe the old saying that if you find out what you're good at, you'll never do a day's work in your life. If you don't enjoy your work, you probably won't succeed. If your goal is simply an easy job, you might get by for a while but will not develop your true potential. There is no substitute for hard work, and it is good to remember that the more efficiently we work, the better we become. While people may be working very hard, they should ask themselves if there is a smarter way to complete the same task. Do you really have to be the one baking the buns at four in the morning?

I learned quickly in business that I had to surround myself with positive people. In Arboretum we sometimes say 'You're being a neg' to people who are being negative and likely to infect others. Many years ago, I made a sign stating 'If you see someone without a smile, give them one of yours' and displayed it in the office and the canteen. It's important to identify inspirational people who drive you to improve. For me, this list would include Tara McCarthy, former CEO of Bord Bia, former President Mary Robinson and the late Feargal Quinn.

As with positivity, I believe happiness is a choice. Martin Seligman, the renowned American psychologist who introduced the concept of positive psychology, says our genes account for 60 percent of happiness and that our attitude accounts for the remaining 40 percent. Being positive, showing love, spreading kindness, showing integrity in all actions, trusting, and learning to give without counting the cost are all powerful tools readily available to each of us. If we use these, it will help us to feel fulfilled. Many seek happiness in someone or something outside themselves. In my opinion, that is a fundamental mistake. Happiness, as they say, is an inside job, regardless of what life throws at us.

***

I love every season of the year. In winter I love to feel the rain on my face and then light a comforting fire and cook a healthy meal. In spring I love to watch the buds burst open on the trees and the hedgerows coming to life. In summer I take time to appreciate my garden and see the benefits of my labour of love. Autumn, of course, is a kaleidoscope of colours – from russet and yellow to orange and red. I count myself blessed that I have such a love and appreciation for everything around me and that I've been privileged to work with nature, plants and wonderful people.

Only in retrospect can we see the pattern of our lives laid out step by step, each one leading progressively to the next. Writing this book has helped me to reflect on my own transformation from a quiet little girl who played hide-and-seek in the ruins of Clonmore Castle in the 1950s to the woman I am today – someone who is always seeking a new dream to follow and who doesn't hide from doing whatever must be done to make it come true. The world I inhabit has changed so much since I was a girl, but in life, as in business, we must embrace that change and remain agile. We must stand our ground when we must but turn the sod on new ground when we can.

I have led a privileged life and could not have wished for a better career and family. My husband Frank and our two sons Fergal and Barry, along with their wives Kim and Lynda and my five adorable grandchildren – Blair, Bebhinn, Frankie, Evan and Liam – and my extended family are my life. My world revolves around my family, community and friends. And, of course, my sweet Arboretum.

Rachel's Reflection

Our beautiful old beech tree is one I admire every day and regard with awe. Its deep roots and strong spreading branches remind me of the growth of Arboretum down through the years – Frank and I being the roots and trunk and Fergal, Barry, Kim, Lynda and our grandchildren being the spreading branches.

FRUITS

Retail Excellence Ireland Lifetime Achievement Award – the third person in 20 years

National retailer of the Year 2021

President Michael D Higgins attended the World Garden Centre Congress in Mansion House

Pat, Jimmy, John, Nancy and Rachel

Arboretum awards night

Rachel and her grandchildren

About *My Tree of Life*

What's remarkable about My Tree of Life *is its energy, vision and warmth. Rachel's deep knowledge of horticulture is undisputed and here she weaves nuggets of information through a tapestry of life story, business growth and personal reflection. A lovely read from a woman of substance.*
Mary Kennedy – Irish TV Personality, former newscaster and writer.

Rachel Doyle is a visionary, an excellent entrepreneur, a renowned horticulturalist, a community leader and much more. But most of all she is a great family woman and a trusted confidant to so many. My Tree of Life *is a delightful read, tracking Rachel's journey from humble beginnings in Clonmore to the presidency of a global organisation. Rachel's honesty and authenticity throughout the book are refreshing. Life's voyage is not without challenges, and Rachel had setbacks too. Still,*

Rachel proved that anything is possible if you have a positive attitude, work hard and surround yourself with like-minded people. The success of the Arboretum on the world stage is a testament to Rachel's vision, passion, strategic thinking, ambition and leadership style. This book is a must-read for anyone looking for inspiration and courage to follow their dream, whether in business or private life. There are nuggets of wisdom on every page.
David Walsh – founder of Netwatch and HaloCare

Authentic, energetic, and energising, yet there is so much more to her. Rachel is a force of nature, a force for good, nurturing and allowing all to flourish. She brings out the best in those she meets, insisting they rise to their potential. She seeks the opportunity in every challenge, in every experience, in every day. She shares insights, knowledge and learning humbly and without hesitation. Generosity the constant theme. It has been

my privilege to have played a very small part in the epic story that is her life and work. Enjoy a fascinating read!
Tara McCarthy – Global Vice President ESG Alltech and former CEO of Bord Bia

My Tree of Life *is the story of a young girl in rural Ireland who dared to follow her dreams and built Arboretum, a nationally recognised, award winning business, based around her passions of horticulture and good locally sourced food. However, this book is so much more than this. Rachel Doyle's story is a story of how she was moulded as a young girl by the influences of her family and local community. Her story will resonate with so many who were raised in Ireland in the second half of the 20th Century and who look back fondly on those seemingly distant days.* My Tree of Life *tells the story of how Rachel's vision to build a business took root despite several setbacks along the way and flourished into today's award-winning and ever-*

growing retail operation. It touches on the highs and lows of this fascinating journey and Rachel's drive, energy and passion shine through. This book goes to show that those who dare to dream can indeed live the dream. Rachel's energy and passion for what she does is indeed an inspiration to us all. I am proud to not only call Rachel a business colleague, but also a friend.

Kevin Neary - M. Phil, M. Inst. D, C Dir. Co-founder and former Managing Director of GameStop Group, Chairman, Non Executive Director and Investor.

Congratulations on an incredible work! A labour of love giving 'voice' to your history, passion, vision, creativity, determination, and so, so much more! Remember 'No two people read the same book'. So many, many people will take and remember different and diverse things from your captivating story with its insight into the social history of Ireland, especially that of Clonmore, and will fill them with a yearning for a treasured life now gone. Others can escape into the wonderful world of 'Rachel's Garden' and languish there to dream and enjoy the exotic vision you weave for us readers! Then your business knowledge and acumen will be a 'bible' for would-be entrepreneurs! Your book is a garden, an orchard, a store of wonderful insights and guidance! Many congratulations on the book of the birth, childhood, teenage years and young adulthood of your 3rd baby... The Arboretum... The Tree of your Life. xxxx

Anne Buggie – friend.

I have to declare my hand here. I have been a massive fan of Rachel Doyle and the incredible businesses that she has built up with her family in Leighlinbridge and Kilquade. I love the Arboretum. As somebody who grew up in rural Ireland, I can relate strongly to much of the life that Rachel Doyle describes in My Tree of Life. *However, there is much more to this book than that.*

Rachel was driven by a combination of human interaction and basic decency, a love of nature and horticulture, and an incredible desire to create something great and succeed in business. This enchanting book describes all of this and much more. For anybody interested in business, nature, social history and the will to succeed against many odds, My Tree of Life *is a must read. It combines business acumen, ambition, humour and an innate decency towards people. Read it and you will benefit enormously from the experience.*
Jim Power – Economist

Rachel Doyle's My Tree of Life *is a well-written book full of vivid and fascinating detail not just about the success of Arboretum but indeed Rachel's own life story. I am both privileged and proud as her brother to pen an acknowledgment in this wonderful book.*

Rachel is a successful business woman, an

entrepreneur, wife, mother and the most generous person you could wish to meet.

I know that I speak for my sister Nancy, brothers Pat and Jim when I say that when any of our family needed help or advice in any way Rachel was always the go-to person.

I still remember all the Sunday evenings driving Rachel back to Termonfeckin Horticultural Collage after her weekend break at home in Carlow. I could never have envisaged where all this would lead, but looking back I suspect Rachel did because she was so determined, so focussed and so sure of the goals she wanted to achieve.

I know that her husband Frank and sons Fergal and Barry are equally proud of Rachel's achievements, not just in founding Arboretum but all the other things she achieved along the way. So I will finish as I started by saying well done Sister, well done Rachel.

John Candy – author of *Rambling Down Memory Lane*

Acknowledgements

A huge thank you to all my family and friends who helped me in any way on this journey. To friends from my school days for clarifying my recollection of life in Clonmore. To my wonderful friends Anne Buggie and Carmel Duignan for your encouragement and support while writing this book and always. To Paul O'Brien and Eilish Rafferty thank you for your patience, advice and guidance, also John MacKenna and Angela Keogh. To the friends who read the book for me: Blaise Brosnan, David Walsh, Kevin Neary, Jim Power, Paddy Byrne, Richie Kavanagh Snr and Pat and John Candy. To Richie Kavanagh Jnr for your sketches of Roots, Trunk, Branches, Leaves and Fruit of my trees. To Lorna Murphy and Darragh Simpson in the office for always being willing to help. To Mark Turner and Marble City Publishing a big thank you. To my own family – you're the best.

Rachel